Robert William Cochran-Patrick

Mediaval Scotland

Robert William Cochran-Patrick

Mediaval Scotland

ISBN/EAN: 9783337341442

Printed in Europe, USA, Canada, Australia, Japan

Cover: Foto ©ninafisch / pixelio.de

More available books at **www.hansebooks.com**

Mediæval Scotland

CHAPTERS ON AGRICULTURE, MANUFACTURES,

FACTORIES, TAXATION, REVENUE, TRADE,

COMMERCE, WEIGHTS AND MEASURES

BY

R. W. COCHRAN-PATRICK
LL.D. Glas., LL B. Cantab., B.A. Edin.

FELLOW OF THE SOCIETY OF ANTIQUARIES ; FELLOW OF THE SOCIETY OF
ANTIQUARIES OF SCOTLAND ; FELLOW OF THE ROYAL SOCIETY OF
ANTIQUARIES OF IRELAND

GLASGOW
JAMES MACLEHOSE AND SONS
Publishers to the University
1892

PREFACE.

THESE chapters, with two exceptions, originally appeared in the *Glasgow Herald* as a series of articles on Early Scotland: and I am much indebted to the proprietors of that paper for their courteous and liberal permission to reprint them. Two articles which appeared in that series, one on the Currency and the other on the Early Mining Industries, are already in a permanent and extended shape in the Introductions to the *Records of the Coinage of Scotland* and *Records of Early Mining in Scotland*, and have not been reprinted.

Two chapters, one on Fisheries and the other on Weights and Measures, now appear for the first time. In connection with the latter I have to express my thanks and obligations to the Lord Provost and Municipal Authorities of Edinburgh, and to the Provost and Municipal Authorities of

Stirling, for permission to engrave the interesting ancient national standards still in their custody; and to the City and Depute-City Clerks of Edinburgh; Mr. Galbraith, the Town Clerk of Stirling; Mr. Ferguson, the Town Clerk of Linlithgow; Mr. Annan, the Town Clerk of Lanark; Mr. A. Smith, Lanark, and Mr. A. Johnston, London, for much valuable information and assistance in connection with the subject.

R. W. COCHRAN-PATRICK.

WOODSIDE, BEITH,
December, 1891.

CONTENTS.

CHAPTER I.
AGRICULTURE, - - - - - - 1

CHAPTER II.
AGRICULTURE, - - - - - - 15

CHAPTER III.
MANUFACTURES, - - - - - - 30

CHAPTER IV.
MANUFACTURES, - - - - - - 48

CHAPTER V.
FISHERIES, - - - - - - - 67

CHAPTER VI.
TAXATION AND REVENUE, - - - - 77

CONTENTS.

CHAPTER VII.

TRADE AND COMMERCE, - - - - 104

CHAPTER VIII.

WEIGHTS AND MEASURES, - - - - 151

ILLUSTRATIONS TO THIS CHAPTER—

The Stirling Standard Stoup, in the Custody of the Burgh of Stirling, - - - iii

Standard Choppin, or Half-pint, in the Custody of the City of Edinburgh, - iii

Standards of the Ell in the Custody of the City of Edinburgh, - - - - 158

Stirling Standard Jug, preserved by the City of Edinburgh, - - - - - 172

APPENDIX, - - - - - - - 173

NOTES, - - - - - - - 183

INDEX, - - - - - - - 189

MEDIÆVAL SCOTLAND.

CHAPTER I.

AGRICULTURE.

In treating this subject it may be convenient to divide the past into certain periods, and deal with each separately, showing as far as possible the methods of cultivation used, the various crops raised, the value received for them, the relations between owners and occupiers, and the burdens imposed in the shape of rent (or payments and services in lieu of rent) for the use of the land. The taxes raised for national and local purposes and laid on land will be dealt with hereafter.

The divisions proposed are (1) the Pre-historic period, coming down to about the close of the seventh century; (2) the Celtic period, coming down to about the close of the twelfth century; (3)

the Early Feudal period, coming down to the reign of James I.; and (4), lastly, the Later Feudal period, closing with the union of the two kingdoms in 1707.

It is necessary to bear in mind concerning the two earlier periods that we are dealing then with four, at least, distinct races, of different origin, different degrees of civilization, and having in many cases different customs. Few things amongst a semi-civilized people are so unchangeable as agricultural customs, and, where the soil and climate permit, they carry to the lands of their settlement the habits of the land of their origin. We may expect, for example, to find the Dalriadic Scots following the Hiberno-Scottish practices, the Norsemen the Norwegian, and so on. Consequently we cannot safely infer that the same state of progress existed all over the country. On the contrary, we find in every period that some parts of the country, peopled by energetic races, were soon far in advance of the others, and that, even among these, considerable differences in agricultural progress are found. To give a complete picture of every part of the country would involve a mass of details which would be out of place on the present occasion, and for the earlier periods indicated above would be almost impossible from lack of evidence. All that is attempted is to give some data which may show points of contrast between the days we live in and the days gone by, and may stimulate some to study for themselves the records of the past.

Commencing with the first of these periods, which extends from an unknown antiquity down to the seventh century, we are in a position to affirm that at the dawn of history, when the Roman invasion took place, agriculture was practically unknown. The earliest historical notices we have of Scotland disclose a state of society apparently without any knowledge of tillage. Cæsar distinctly says that the inhabitants did not resort to the cultivation of the soil for food, but were dependent upon their cattle and the flesh of animals slain in hunting. And so late as the third century Dion Cassius, according to his abridger, Xifiline, confirmed the fact that the early Caledonians lived up to that date only by pasturage and the chase.

How long this condition of things existed we have no means of ascertaining. Our knowledge of the Romano-British period, and the three centuries immediately succeeding it, is so scanty that it is impossible to dogmatize in the absence of trustworthy evidence. Were conjecture admissible when dealing with historical matters it might be surmised that the Romans would hardly have occupied the country so long as they did without introducing cropping of some kind. But there is no direct evidence of it, so far at least as Scotland is concerned. "Querns," the ancient stone handmills, have been found in the crannogs of Ayrshire, and charred grain (bere and oats) in the Broch of Dunbeath. But these may have been left by the last inhabitants, possibly in comparatively recent times. The famous miracle of S. Ninian about the leeks would show that garden herbs were known and cultivated in the beginning of the fifth century. But the only life we now have of the apostle of Galloway was written by Ailred in the twelfth century, though he professes to write from a very ancient original, and may have recorded a traditional fact. When we come to Adamnan's life of S. Columba we are entitled to believe that agriculture of a certain sort was practised (at least amongst the Dalriadic Scots) in the seventh century, if not actually during the saint's life, a hundred years earlier. It is related by his biographer that Columba, when in Iona, having taken from a cottar some bundles of twigs to wattle a house, sent him in return six measures of barley, which, though not sown till the 13th of June, were reaped in the beginning of August. Various other agricultural operations are noticed in the same work. Ploughing and sowing occur in the 45th chapter of the second book; harvest work in the 29th chapter of the first book; corn-grinding in the 22nd chapter of the first book; and one of the last earthly deeds of the saint was to bless the barn of the family of Iona, and two heaps of winnowed corn which were in it. According to Dr. O'Donovan, cereal crops were known in Ireland long previous to the introduction of Christianity; and the Scots of Dalriada may have brought their agricultural knowledge with them.

Joceline, in his life of S. Kentigern (or Mungo), of Glasgow, records a miracle which shows that oxen were used for ploughing; for he relates how the holy man, not having any cattle, would have had to let his land lie fallow had not a stag and a wolf miraculously come out of a wood and ploughed nine acres for him. But again in this case Joceline wrote centuries after Mungo slept with the other 654 saints in the cemetery of "Glasghu"; and probably the correct historical inference is that oxen were used for agricultural tillage in the twelfth century, when the life was written.

We may, therefore, reasonably conclude that on the introduction of Christianity into Scotland agriculture was practised, though we cannot fix the exact period of its introduction. Neither can we say much regarding the methods practised nor the results obtained. But it is highly probable that the system which we find in operation in the immediately succeeding period existed from a much earlier time, and was the immediate development of pre-historic rural economy.

During the Celtic period our knowledge of agricultural methods is still very defective, though we learn something of the state of land tenure and cultivation from occasional notices in the earlier chronicles now made accessible, and from the close analogy which exists between the customs of the various branches of the Celtic race. We find that at this period, for example, the social unit both of the Gaelic and Cymric peoples was not the individual or the family, but the tribe. The territory of the tribe (the Irish *tuath*) was held partly in severalty (by the *rig* and *flaths* in Ireland) and partly in common by the rest of the community. In Celtic Scotland a somewhat similar state of matters is found. The tribes occupied their territories in the following manner :— The arable tribe land was distributed at certain intervals among the free tribesmen. The pastoral tribe land was held in common. The inheritance land was held by the headmen as individual property by blood descent. Of these chiefs there were two sorts, one getting their position by descent, the other by accumulations of property. They cultivated their estates either by bond men or by free tenants on a tenure, of which steelbow (or *stuht*) is a survival. Strangers in blood to the tribe often joined a sept, and received a portion from the chief, giving in return their sword-service and customary dues. Besides the tribe land and the inheritance land, each clan gave a portion of its territory for the support of the office-bearers, the Toisech, the Tanist, the Filé, and the Brehon, and, after the introduction of Christianity, to the Saggart or priest. The homestead was composed of a dwelling-house, ox stall, hog sty, a sheep pen, and a calf-house, and was surrounded by an earthen rampart, and called usually a *Rath*. Constant reference to these is made in early Scottish charters. Thus in the Chartulary of Scone we have a grant to the Abbey of the Church of Logymahedd, with the Rath "qua est caput comitatus." In the Chartulary of Moray we have a notice of the Rath of Kingussie. In the Chartulary of Arbroath we find the Rath of the territory of Katerlyn mentioned. This homestead or *Rath* was the unit of which the aggregate made up the tribe.

These tuaths or tribes are found with us both among the Northern Picts and the Dalriadac Scots of the Western Highlands. The notices in the ancient tract quoted by Mr. Skene, the Amra-Choluim-Chilli, show that in the time of Columba these tribal settlements existed amongst the Dalriads and the heathen Picts. For example, we find the land north of the Clyde occupied by three tribes— the Cinel Gabran, Cinel Angus, and the Cinel Lorn. The Cinel Gabran occupied Kintyre, Arran, and Bute, and had 560 homesteads, with 20 houses each; the Cinel Angus possessed Isla and Jura, and had

430 homesteads; and the Cinel Lorn peopled the district of that name, and had 420 homesteads.

We find traces of tribes also in Galloway. In the charter-room of the Marquess of Ailsa at Culzean there is a confirmation in 1276 of a charter by Neil of Carrick to Roland of Carrick, of "Kenkenol," or the right of being head of the tribe or kin. The tenants of these tribes paid their rent in services or in kind, for it must be remembered there was no coined money in Scotland till the time of David I. And of these burdens in lieu of rent there were at this time four, viz.—Cain, Conveth, Feacht, and Sluaged. The first two were payments in kind, the others were personal service. We find these frequently mentioned in the chartularies and in early charters. Thus King David granted to the Church of Glasgow the tithe of his "Can" of Strathgrif, Cunningham, Kyle, and Carrick.

Can or *Cain* was a portion of the produce of the land, and was rendered in grain from arable farms, and in stock from pasture land. It was paid by the occupiers of the soil to the owner in every part of Scotland down to the feudal period, and long after where feudal tenure did not prevail.

Conveth was founded on the original right which the leaders of the Celtic tribe had to be supported by their followers, and it finally became a fixed contribution on each plough-gate of land. In the Chartulary of Scone we find a grant from Malcolm IV. to the abbey at the Feast of All Saints, for their *conveth*, of 1 cow and 2 pigs, some meal and oats, 10 hens, 200 eggs, 10 bundles of candles, 4 lb. of soap, and 20 half-meales of cheese. In the Western Highlands this rent was called the " Cuddicke," and is mentioned in the Western Islands late on in the fifteenth century, and is found later still in Atholl. It is sometimes also called " *Conyou*," under which form it occurs in a contract between the Bishop of the Isles and Lauchlan M'Lean of Dowart in 1580. A somewhat similar rent, called " *Sorryn*," was of old exacted in Galloway.

The "*Feacht*" and "*Siuaged*" were obligations of personal service to follow the head of the tribe in expeditions and wars, and in Scotland were laid on the davoch of land. These ancient Celtic obligations appear in later times to be what is called in old charters " Scottish service," or " expedition and hosting."

Such were the obligations of the occupiers and tillers of the ground from the earliest dawn of authentic record down to the close of the Celtic period in the eleventh century.

Coming now to the earlier feudal period, we glean our chief information as to the state of rural economy mostly from the chartularies and registers of the great religious houses. From these we can gather a tolerably exact account of the state of agriculture from the eleventh to the close of the thirteenth centuries. During this period we cannot trace any legal enactments, but there is no doubt that the force of custom, in itself almost stronger in rude nations than that of law, existed, and stereotyped what men were to do with regard to the cultivation of the soil.

It is hardly necessary to say that the monks were the great promoters and encouragers of agriculture. One of the earliest sources of knowledge we have is a rental of the possessions of the Abbey of Kelso, drawn up in 1290.

From it we find that in each principal district there was a "grange," or abbey homestead. It was usually under the charge of a lay brother of the convent, or sometimes of one of the monks, and included the store-house for the implements, the byres for cattle, the home of the "*carles*," and the granary of the domain, or "mains." The *carles* (nativi, or serfs) were really bondmen, who belonged to the land and went with it. Outside the "*grange*" dwelt the "*cottarii*," or cottars, occupying a hamlet, or "town," with from one to nine acres each of land, for which they paid a money rent and certain services. Then came the "*husbandi*," or "*malars*," or farmers, renting a "*husbandland.*" This husbandland was generally two *oxgates* of land, each 13 acres, "where plough and scythe could gang." Four husbandmen occupied together a *plough-gate*, equal to 104 acres, and had a common plough to which each contributed two oxen. These were neighbours, and strict rules of good fellowship were laid down, and, when necessary, enforced by the "*birley men*" chosen by themselves.

As early as 1185 there were enclosed fields for cultivation, for in that year Robert Avenel gave to the monks of Melrose certain lands in Upper Eskdale, and the privilege of hunting and hawking without prejudice to the enclosures.

When we come to consider the return from land during this period we have to deal with the important factor of money payments as well as services and payments in kind. And we also find a very great advance in civilization and in the methods of agriculture. The monastic chartularies and rentals give some idea of the burdens then imposed on tenants. One example may serve as a sort of guide. On the barony of Bolden the monks had twenty-eight husbandlands. Each paid eighty sterlings or silver pennies annually as silver rent, and the following services besides, viz., the whole family gave four days' reaping in harvest, one day carrying peats, a man and a horse to and from Berwick once a year, an acre and a half's ploughing and one day's harrowing, a man at sheep-washing and one at sheep-shearing, and one day's work with a waggon at harvest time. Besides these, each farmer had to take the abbot's wool to the abbey and pay a *reck-hen* at Christmas. In addition to the 28 principal farmers there were 36 cottars, 1 miller, and 4 brewers. Each of the cottages had half an acre of land. The cottars rendered certain services and paid in whole 668 sterlings. The mill rented for 8 merks, and the four brew-houses paid 120 sterlings yearly.

We find that they produced oats, wheat, barley, pease, and beans. There is very little mention of rye. Lint paid teind in the reign of William the Lion in Moray. Oats were the main crop, furnishing both meal and malt. Much larger quantities were grown than might be expected. In 1300 the cavalry of Edward of England, returning from Galloway, when near Dornoch, in Dumfriesshire, passed through the growing crops of a proprietor there, who claimed damages for 80 acres of oats injured. The claim was admitted, and a sum of 5,760 sterlings paid him as damages, or at the rate of 72 per acre. Barley malt is very rare, and high in price. In 1300 oats and oat malt were 42 sterlings a quarter, and barley malt 52; wheat was 84 sterlings the quarter, beans 60 sterlings, and pease 33 sterlings. The usual price for a chalder of oats was a merk (160 sterlings) though sometimes it rose as high as 240 sterlings; while that of barley was a merk, though sometimes it fell to 120 sterlings.

Cheese was made in considerable quantities at an early period. Malcolm IV. granted to the monks of Melrose a place at Cumbesley to build a dairy for 100 cows.

We need only refer to one more authority of this sort for the same period. In the venerable Chartulary of Melrose there are many most interesting incidental notices throwing light on rural affairs down to the death of Alexander III. We find strict rules laid down for the protection of growing corn and hay meadows. We find wheat cultivated, and wheaten bread used on holidays. Roads—in some cases at least suitable for wheel vehicles—as appears from the penalty for trespassing on private roads, being fixed at a penny for a four-wheeled and a halfpenny for a two-wheeled waggon —were frequent, and wheeled conveyances in common use. Mills driven by wind or water were used for grinding corn, though the old "quern" still held its own in some districts.

With regard to stock, it appears from a record in the same chartulary that the monks in 1247 bought from Patrick of Dunbar his stud of horses and brood mares for 8,000 silver pennies, a very large sum in those days. Of sheep the abbey had immense flocks. Three flocks of wedders, of 500 each, were pastured near Hart's-head in Haddington. From Roland of Galloway they had pasturage for 700 ewes with their followers of two years, for 49 cows similarly attended, a bull, 40 oxen, 8 horses, and 4 swine with their followers for three years. In Wedale they grazed 7 score cattle and 500 sheep, and on Primside 400 sheep.

Minute and-careful arrangements are laid down for the folds and fanks, the shepherds, separation of pastures, removal of stock at various times of the year, etc. The shepherds in some cases had movable lodges with them.

In this period we find for the first time positive laws relating to the land and agriculture. In the year 1214 bondsmen were to begin to plough and sow 15 days before the Feast of the Purification. And, to encourage agriculture, Alexander II. in the same Parliament ordered every person who possessed more than four cows to rent land and plough it with the cattle; and those who had fewer cattle were to till it by hand labour, under certain pains and penalties.

And in a fragment of uncertain date it is laid down that if a tenant puts " gule " (a noxious weed not unknown at the present day) in the land he is to be punished as if he had led an enemy into the country—that is apparently with death. Should it be owing to the carelessness of a bondager, he shall pay a sheep for every plant of it, and clean the land besides.

CHAPTER II.

AGRICULTURE.

WE are now in a position to get some idea of the prices of the various agricultural products. In 1259 Fordun relates that there was a great famine in Scotland, so that the boll of meal sold for 48 sterlings or silver pennies, evidently a very extreme price. In 1296 the army of Edward of England wasted and destroyed certain crops, the property of the Priory of Coldstream. The damage was estimated by the monks at 48 quarters of wheat, each quarter priced at 60 silver pennies; 40 quarters of rye, at 48 silver pennies; 56 quarters of barley, at 60 silver pennies; 80 quarters of oats, at 24 silver pennies. Sheep were estimated at 8 sterlings; oxen and cows, at 36 each; pigs, at 10; work horses, at 60 each. To make up the loss certain amounts of wheat, beans, and malt were sent by the English King, and the monks valued his wheat at 120 sterlings the quarter, the beans at 92 sterlings, and the malt at 84 sterlings. In a tack by the Abbot of Aberbrothock in 1314 a cow is valued at 60 silver pennies, and an ox, in 1317, at 80 silver pennies.

A very important change in the relationship between owners and occupiers of land also begins now to make its appearance. Leases or written agreements, giving to the cultivators a legal security for a defined period on certain conditions, are much earlier than is commonly supposed. They occur in the twelfth and thirteenth centuries, were well known in the fourteenth, and the common custom, in civilized Scotland, in the fifteenth and sixteenth. In 1190, Alan, son of Walter the Stewart, approved a lease by the monks of Kelso to his men of Innerwich of certain lands for thirty-three years. Many others are mentioned in the chartularies. One occurs in 1312, entered into between the Abbot of Scone and Hay of Leys. The abbot sets the lands of Balgarvie for thirty years, the rent at first being 160 silver pennies, rising 80 sterlings per annum for six years; 480 sterlings from the seventh to the twelfth year; 640 from the twelfth to the twentieth; and 800 sterlings from the twentieth to the thirtieth. The tenant was to erect his buildings, and to have power to sublet. In all these cases the money rent was in addition to the usual and customary suits and services. Somewhat later we find the Crown lands managed by commissioners, whose reports are preserved in the Register House from 1480. Leases were granted for three, five, seven, thirteen, and nineteen years. The new lease was generally given two years before the expiry of the old one. A "grassum"[1] of one year's rent was paid for the lease, and in some cases another year's rent as entry money.

Some very curious and interesting early leases are preserved in a rental book of the Abbey of Cupar, extending from 1443 to 1538. The leases usually last from five to seven years, though some are for longer periods, as nineteen years, and some are for life. The rents were payable in money, service, and kind. The tenants could sub-let small portions to labourers. The cottars were bound to have enclosures for kail, apparently for sanitary reasons. Strict rules were laid down for cutting peats, irrigating pastures, reclaiming marsh land, and the rotation of crops. Every tenant was to "win the land fra guld."[2] In 1462 manure seems to have been regularly employed on the barley fields. In a lease of 1558 Robert Alexander was promised all the dung from the stables, with the ashes and dust from the convent workshops and courts, for manuring his land. After 1468 the leases contain provisions for planting trees, such as ash, sauchs,[3] and osiers.

Broom plantations were made for the "conies," and were under the charge of a special officer of the abbey. The woods also were protected, and placed under a forester. In 1475 the leases contain clauses that the tenants were to be respectable in their clothing—a provision made by Act of Parliament in 1429, which prohibited farmers from wearing ragged garments.

The proprietor then made and repaired the houses, but the tenant seems to have kept them up during his lease. A house and three acres of land were let in 1453 at a yearly rent of 120 sterlings. Another, with four acres, at 192 sterlings and the services of two reapers. Security was in some cases taken for the rent, and also for the just fulfilment of the conditions. Tenants were fined by the abbot for destroying the wood, and had also to keep up and restore fences. From one of the extracts it would appear that husbandmen and cottars were regulated by different customs. In the lease of the Grange of Balbrogy, in 1468, it is stipulated that those holding the middle ploughgate[4] should answer to the monastery in the law of husbandmen, but regarding fuel they shall stand as cottars. Another lease, in 1466, has the curious provision that the tenant, John Barbur, who was evidently suffering from some disease, probably leprosy, should, after the first year's sowing, depart from his wife and family to a place suitable for his infirmity, and not thereafter return to any suspected communication with the place. In 1468 another lease contains provisions for draining the moss of Syoks, by a sufficient aqueduct. This same tenant of Syoks, one Dic Scot, had a lease for five years, with this curious provision "that if he shall not be sober and temperate, preserving more strictly a kindly intercourse with his neighbours and relatives," his lease was to be of no avail. Another tenant, John Crochat, in 1470, is obliged to promise on oath to preserve a kindly and lawful neighbourhood. After an Act of Parliament in 1472, regulating the rotation of crops, we find John Spark, tenant of little Perth, is taken bound to adhere to the state regulations in sowing wheat, pease, rye, and beans, failing which he is to forfeit his lease.

The "cuningar," or rabbit warren was under the charge of a special officer, who in 1475 was one Gilbert Ray. A lease of two acres of ground, with pasturage, free of rent, was given to him for looking after the vermin. A curious provision is inserted in some of the leases about 1478. Walter Dog gets a lease of Kyncrech in that year, and one of the conditions is, "he shall never murmur abbot nor convent about his lease," or else freely "gie it our." Probably the fathers had been having complaints. In 1541 a fowler appears, who was allowed to kill all sorts of wild fowl on condition that he delivered them to the abbey, receiving certain payments for each.

Ordinary disputes were settled by oversmen, or "birley men," in each district. The monastery had a ground officer on each estate, to see that the conditions of the tacks were punctually and faithfully carried out.

The moorland tenants were bound to keep dogs to hunt the wolves, which seem to have committed great ravages on the flocks.

The land was divided into "*in field*" land, that is, arable, and "*out field*," or unreclaimed. "*Shepherdland*" seems to have been generally hill pasturage, to which the sheep were sent at suitable seasons.

Leases were forfeited by conviction for theft, adultery, reset of stolen goods, by encouraging too many cottars, by unneighbourly or intemperate conduct, by failure of proper rotation of crops, by allowing weeds, and by non-payment of rent or services.

Various Acts of Parliament were introduced for the purpose of encouraging agriculture during this period. In 1366 we find a statute forbidding the horses of followers of the king's officers doing damage to the crops or growing hay under severe penalties, and in 1481 the same statute was re-enacted and confirmed. Great damage being done to the crops by rooks, Parliament in 1424 ordered the young crows to be destroyed; and if any nests were found undestroyed at Beltane,[5] the trees on which they were were to be cut down, and a fine of 60 pence imposed on the owner of the trees. This Act was extended in 1457 to all kinds of destructive birds. Another Act of 1424 provided that every labourer was either to be the joint owner of an ox fit to go in the plough, or, if not, he was to dig seven square feet of ground every day, or to pay a fine equal to the full value of an ox. Two years later another Act was passed requiring every tenant who was the owner of a plough team of oxen to sow yearly at least a firlot⁶ of wheat, half a firlot of pease, and forty beans; or failing, to forfeit 120 pence. Similarly, owners of land, in their own occupation, were to sow in proportion, or be fined 480 pence in default, and a similar sum for each of their tenants who neglected to sow his proportion.

A very important Act was passed in 1449. In order to encourage agricultural tenants, it was then enacted that whoever had a written lease could not be interfered with or put out of his holding if he fulfilled the conditions of his agreement, even though the land was sold. A special clause was inserted providing that tenants on Church lands falling to the Crown should not thereby be disturbed. By another Act of the same date every farmer was prohibited from having stacks of corn in his yard after 25th December of each year: and a further provision in 1452 ordered all grain to be threshed before the end of May.

We get some insight into the state of agriculture during the later feudal period from a rental of the Bishopric of Aberdeen in 1511.

From this it appears that the average rent of a ploughgate of land in that district was £3 7s. 9d. of *silver maill* or money rent; one year's rent as "grassum"; 20d. for commuted services, 1 firlot of oats, 1 firlot of malt, 1 firlot of meal, ¼ of a mart, 1 sheep, ¼ of a kid, 5 capons, 5 fowls, 4 moor-fowl, and 1 pig from the mill, with 2 stones of cheese from each pastoral holding. The crofters were bound to build one rood of the fold for every cow possessed. Each paid 9s. 9d. of *silver maill*, 1 firlot of barley, and 10 fowls. Tenants were bound to build, but in some cases were allowed the cost.

Similar provisions are found on a barony in the same district in 1532. The ploughgate of land was usually let to four tenants, each sending two oxen to help to drag the common plough. Each plough paid on the average 32 bolls of victual, or a money rent of from £2 to £3 Scots besides services and customs, use and wont.

It is difficult to give an accurate idea of the value of agricultural produce during this period, owing to the unsettled state of the country, the not infrequent occurrence of years of exceptional scarcity, and the constant changes in the value of money. From the

Act. Dom. Auditorum[7] (1466 to 1494) we get a wide range of prices. Meal varies from 10s. to 20s. the boll;[8] oats, from 2s. to 11s. the boll; pease, about 13s. 4d. the boll; sheep range from 3s. to 6s. 8d. each; cows and oxen, from 20s. to 40s. each; and horses, from £2 to £10 each. The will of Giles Blair, Lady Row, executed in 1530, gives some idea of Ayrshire prices at that time. Her 61 cows are valued over head at 2 merks[9] each; oxen, at 30s. each; sheep, at 5s. each; bere and meal, 12s. the boll; and oats, 6s. the boll.

At a later date the judicial records of Renfrewshire show the prices of agricultural produce to be as follow :—

Bere, the boll, 1687	£7	12	6	Scots.
Oats ,, ,,	9	12	0	,,
Oatmeal ,, ,,	7	16	2	,,
Butter, the cwt., 1687	21	4	0	,,
Cheese, the stone, 1696	4	13	0	,,
Wool, the stone, 1698	4	0	0	,,
Cows, each, 1687	17	19	0	,,
Sheep ,, ,,	3	0	0	,,

The Parliamentary enactments relating to agricultural holdings from the reign of James II. to the close of the national independence of Scotland are both numerous and important.

In 1457 tenants were required to plant trees near their steadings; hedges round their fields; and broom, for what purpose is not stated. A series of

Acts commencing in 1503 prohibited oxen, horses, or other gear pertaining to the plough from being pounded or distrained for debt, if the debtor had any other goods or lands. It was made illegal in 1535 to assess any part of the payment of special grants made by Parliament to the Crown on tenants or labourers of the ground. Owing to the injury done to the corn, hay, and enclosures of poor tenants by riders coming to do their military service, it was enacted in 1540 that no one except the great barons should come on horseback to the trysting place of the king's army. A great dearth of victual took place in the year 1562, and in 1563 Parliament ordered all persons of whatever degree to thresh their corn and sell it at once ; and any stacks found standing on the 10th of July were to be confiscated. This Act was to last for the crops of 1563, 1564, and 1565. The maiming of cattle and the cutting or injuring of ploughs or ploughing gear, and the destruction of growing corn or wood were punished with death by an Act of 1587.

The duties of farm servants were laid down by an Act of 1621. After reciting the evils which had arisen from agricultural labourers either refusing to be hired at all without " great and extraordinary " wages, or engaging only from Martinmas to Whitsunday, and then " casting themselves loose " from their engagements at a time when much farm-work, such as cutting peats, etc., had to be done, it was provided that no farm servant should leave his employment at Whitsunday unless he could prove he was *fee'd*[10] to some other situation; and if not he was to be compelled to return to the farm and serve for such wages as had formerly been agreed on. In 1645 a Frenchman applied to Parliament for leave to introduce the cultivation of Indian corn into this country, but the result of his experiment is not recorded. Grain and cattle were permitted to be exported by an Act of 1662. And between 1685 and 1703 various enactments occur encouraging the cultivation of pease and beans, regulating winter herding, prohibiting butchers from having more than one acre as grazing, under penalty of a fine of £100 and forfeiture of the cattle grazed, and for improving crops by applying lime to the fields.

In the beginning of the seventeenth century we get a good idea of the rural economy of the time from a rental of the Gordon estates, taken in 1600, and printed by the Spalding Club.

The agricultural holdings are generally about two ploughgates each and set to eight tenants. A small silver maill was paid; but the bulk of the rent (called ferme) was rendered in kind—viz., certain bolls of oatmeal and bear, besides "customs," such as the "reek-hen," a mart, poultry, etc. Professor Innes, in his "Legal Antiquities," has summed up and averaged the rent for every ploughgate in the parish of Bellie as £2 8s. for silver maill, 20 bolls of ferme victual, 1½ bolls of multure, bear, etc., besides customs and carriages.

The leases were usually from five to six years, though it is highly probable these varied according to the class of tenants. At a somewhat later period we find several distinct classes of rural occupiers. These were the " Tacksmen," or tenants with leases ; next in importance were the " Bowers," who farmed milk " kye " and their grass, and the " Steel Bowers," who received stock and cattle along with their farms. After these come the " Pendiclers," who had a small quantity of land, generally held from the chief tenant or tacksman ; and " Cottars," who had a house and portion of land, and who worked with the farmer, but had no cattle, and got their tillage work done by the tenant. The " Crofters " differed from cottars in that their arable land was not subject to the tenant's pleasure, and they had their cattle herded and pastured with the tacksman. Lastly, we find the " Dryhouse Cottars," who had nothing but a hut and a kailyard.

We get a still later glimpse of agricultural life in the seventeenth century, and in a different part of the country, from the Corshill Baron court book, recently printed by the Ayr and Galloway Archæological Association. This record began prior to

1590, and continues down to 1719, but the earlier portion has been lost, and the existing roll begins in 1666. The court was constituted by the Laird of the Barony of Corshill, in Stewarton parish, Ayrshire, the whole tenants and feuars lawfully summoned, the "Bailie" appointed by the Baron (who presided as judge), the "Baron Officer" and the "Dempster," who pronounced the "doom" of the court. The Officer was appointed by the Baron, "with consent of the tennentis of the ground." The Laird and the Bailie, "with consent of the ground," appointed also certain persons as "birleymen,"[11] whose duty was to keep good neighbourhood and solve disputes referred to them. The court in certain cases also fixed on two "honest men," to whose judgment disputants agreed to defer. Tenants who were absent were fined for their contumacy, in one case as high as £4 Scots.

The greater portion of the cases dealt with belonged to the every-day life of an agricultural community. The miller complained about those who abstracted the corn from the mill to which they were "thirled,"[12] and the offenders had to pay the "multures,"[13] with 6s. 8d. Scots in addition as expenses. Sub-tenants who had taken pasturage from the tenants sometimes refused to pay the "grass maill," and were brought up and ordained to pay. The "merchant at the Kirk" (of Stewarton) continually complained that he was not paid his just debts, and got decrees in his favour. Janet Harper pursued Margate Stirling in that she took away peats out of the moss which belonged to the said Janet. Disputes about bargains, about the quality of stock or crop sold, about fences, about the damage done by cattle breaking into crop land, and such like matters seem to have chiefly occupied the attention of the court. From time to time Acts were made and promulgated by the Bailie with consent of the tenants, such as against any one breaking fences or trees, or stealing fruit or cutting broom, or steeping lint in running water, or killing "reid"[14] fish, or shooting hares, or wild fowl, or burning moss out of season. The court also regulated weights and measures, and, from time to time, imposed as a school rate 22s. out of every £100 Scots of valuation. In one case they compelled the payment of arrears of school fees. "Flyting"[15] women who annoyed their neighbours were brought up and smartly dealt with. Occasionally more serious crimes occur. Margaret Bryson in Beith stole James Wylie's bonnet, and was fined 50 pennies Scots. George Harbiesone "aggressed" and fell upon Hugh Bicket in Hareshaw, and "for blood and battery and breaking of his leg" had to pay £50 Scots, of which the aforesaid Hugh got £45 "for the cureing of his leg." For "molesting the clerk" of the court, John

Picken was fined summarily £5. The shoemaker got into trouble for abusing Sir David Cunningham, yr. of Corshill, " at ane very heigh rate," and calling him names, " with many grievous oaths and sic like," for which he had to pay £20 Scots.

Throughout the whole of this period agriculture was in a very bad state. The crops were poor, the cultivation miserable, and prices very bad. The improvements which were soon to take place lie outside the period we are dealing with. The origin and progress of these improvements are extremely interesting, and we may return to them on some future occasion.

In conclusion, and reviewing the whole history of agriculture from the dawn of authentic record to the Union, the most prosperous times were undoubtedly the reigns of Alexander II. and III. The wars of independence and the unhappy intestine feuds which disturbed and convulsed the whole country retarded the growth of every sort of progress, and agricultural interests were among the first to suffer.

CHAPTER III.

MANUFACTURES.

To those who believe that the national greatness of this country depends in no small measure on the prosperity of its manufacturing and commercial industries, it will not be without interest to trace the origin and growth of these amongst ourselves. And the most prominent point in the history of early Scottish manufactures is the persistent national desire to promote and develop them. Often the means adopted seem to our ideas to be erroneous, and very often they fail. But the object aimed at was never lost sight of. From the days when William the Lion founded his royal burghs with practically exclusive monopolies of manufactures and commerce in order to encourage trade, to the times when James VI. crowded the Statute Books with Acts of Parliament for the same purpose, the one idea was to stimulate by every means commercial enterprise.

It would be impossible within the compass of the present work to give in detail the rise of manufactures in each burgh or district. All we propose is to note the various steps which were taken from time to time by public authority to promote commercial interests, and to trace as far as possible the results achieved.

During the prehistoric ages our knowledge of the arts and industries of the early tribes is extremely limited. It would be rash to assume that absolute barbarism prevailed in every part of the country and at all periods. Every now and then some relic of the forgotten past turns up which shows a technical skill and artistic knowledge which can hardly be reconciled with the commonly received notions of the state of the primitive inhabitants of this country. Celtic traditions point to the very high antiquity, and to a very remarkable development, of native industries. Fifteen centuries before the Christian era, Tigherumas Mac Ollaig was the first, according to these venerable legends, to put colours into cloth and ornamental borders to garments. The catalogue of the possessions of Ailill and Medbh given in the ancient tale of the Táin Bo Chuailgne enumerates raiment of crimson, blue, black, green, yellow, speckled, grey, and striped and other colours not easily identified. The costumes of the chiefs described in the same story also display a wonderful variety of manufactured stuffs. Conchobar Mac

Nessa wore a crimson five-folding fuan or tunic with a shirt of cloth of gold. Another warrior, Munremur Mac Gercin, was attired in a dark long-wooled cloak and a shirt of striped silk. Amargin Mac Ecelsalach shone conspicuous among the clans in a blue five bordered shirt, with carved clasps of white bronze (*findruine*) and buttons of gold, and "a cloak mottled with the splendour of all the most beautiful colours." From the Brehon Laws and the Book of Rights, published by the Celtic Society in 1847, Professor Eugene O'Curry has made out the complete process of the manufacture and dyeing of the textiles used by the ancient Celts. Embroidery and needlework were also carried to a high pitch of perfection. S. Columb Cillé had an embroideress named Coca, as is recorded in the Feilire Aenghuis, who rests in Cillé Choca (now Kilcock) in Kildare.

Whatever we may think of these traditions, it is impossible to doubt the evidence of existing relics. From the perishable nature of the materials it would be an occurrence of the most extreme rarity to find— except, perhaps, in the soil and climate of Egypt— textile fabrics in existence even of a period much later than those claimed by the Celtic annals. But when we look at some of the sculptured stones and at the work on many of the gold and silver ornaments of the prehistoric ages, and, above all, at the illuminations on some of the early Celtic manuscripts such as the Book of Kells, executed probably in the sixth or seventh century, we must admit an intellectual culture far in excess of what might have been expected. It is remarkable that the Scots of Dalriada do not seem to have brought with them from their Ulster homes arts and culture which undoubtedly flourished there, though probably at a later period than that assigned by their traditions. And it is still more curious that the same race remained inert and unmoved by the various influences which in other parts of Scotland began to stimulate commercial enterprise. On the other hand, the Saxon settlers, if they did not leave a high civilization behind them, possessed a capability for future development, which soon began to tell on national progress. Of the state of the native Caledonian tribes we can say very little. But whenever these various races began to be blended in one nationality, and settled down under a recognized government, the latent energies immediately, though gradually, came into activity, and ultimately have risen into the first rank.

Probably the oldest existing specimen of early Scottish textile manufacture is a garment preserved in the National Museum of Antiquities in Edinburgh, which was found many years ago in a prehistoric grave in Orkney. It is impossible to assign a date to it, as from the extreme rarity of such finds we have

c

no means of comparison. Even when history begins, a long period elapses before any notice is taken of manufactures of any kind. During the century and a half of peace and prosperity which closed with the death of Alexander III. there is some ground for believing that textile manufactures existed to a certain extent in this country. In the " Leges Burgorum," or laws of the burghs of Scotland, we find the 22nd law prohibiting any one but a burgess from making cloth or dyeing it. Part of this ancient code dates back to the reign of David I. In the original Cartulary of Glasgow, a volume of venerable antiquity, written in a hand of the thirteenth century is a little capitular, giving the privileges of the burghs at that period. The second of these provides that no one without the burgh shall presume to make cloth, on pain of the king's amercement unforgiven—an enactment probably of the reign of William the Lion. In the charter granted by the same king to the city of Perth all manufacture of cloth in the sheriffdom is prohibited except by those who were burgesses of that royal and favoured town. Similar provisions exist in the charters granted during the same reign to Aberdeen and the burgh and shire of Inverness. And it is to this period and to the policy of William the Lion that we must date the exclusive privileges of the burghs which can be traced down to a very much later time.

In 1398 cloth exported to foreign parts was to pay 2s. of custom in the pound. Woollen cloth was to be measured by the rig [16] and not by the selvidge [17] in 1469.

The weavers of Edinburgh received a seal of cause [18] in 1475. In 1491 six weavers were tried by the magistrates of Dunfermline. Woollen cloth manufactured in Scotland was exported to Amsterdam in 1495. The "Walkers" [19] of Edinburgh were incorporated in 1500. The Convention of Royal Burghs sitting at Edinburgh in 1529 ordered that " na manner of walcar nor wobster [20] mak ony claith of thar awin to sell agane." In 1473 the importation of cloth from England was prohibited, the reason assigned being that the Scotch only got cloth, which they could make at home, for their salmon and other fish, instead of gold and silver as formerly ; and ten years later a duty of 4 oz. of standard silver was imposed on every " serplath " [21] of cloth brought into the country by the merchants. In 1540 the Parliament of Scotland enacted that in every burgh there should be a qualified man chosen to seal all cloth in token of its good quality ; and if any cloth of inferior sort was found, half of the goods of the offender were to be forfeited to the King, and the other half to the burgh. It would be interesting to know if any of these old seals, probably of lead, are still in existence. In the

Parliament of 1567 it was provided that the old Acts anent "wobsters," "walkers," and makers of white cloth were to be put in force, with this addition, that care was to be taken that the cloth was not "flokkit," or, in other words, with the nap raised or improperly thickened. In order to promote woollen manufactures and to give employment to poor persons it was forbidden in 1581 to export wool out of the country.

Shortly after this period James VI. made a strong effort to improve native industries, and among other expedients three skilled workmen from the Low Countries named John Gardin, Philip Fermant, and John Banko were brought to Scotland for the purpose of establishing a textile manufactory. They were engaged to remain in the country for five years, and were to be accompanied by thirty attendants, including a skilled "litster" or dyer. They were to manufacture as good cloth as was made in Flanders, Holland, or England, and of the same patterns and quality; and they were further bound to teach Scottish born apprentices all the secrets of their trade. Nicolas Vduart, burgess of Edinburgh, was appointed overseer of the factory, and was ordered to see that the strangers had everything provided for them, including a wright to set up their looms. Each piece of cloth of satisfactory quality was to be stamped, and to have a seal of lead attached to it. They were to manufacture "serges," [22] "growgrams," [23] "bombesies," [24] "stemmingis," [25] "beyis," [26] fustians, bed covers, and other fabrics; they were to have a proper place in Edinburgh, and other principal towns, for selling their goods on market days; all necessary materials for their machinery were to be supplied free; they were to be exempt from all taxation and public burdens, and were to have, if they required, a church and minister of their own. In spite of this care for their spiritual welfare the strangers were evidently not beyond the supervision of the clergy of the "gude toon" of Edinburgh. For in 1588 it is recorded in the records of the burgh that "be ressoun of the difference in materis of relligion betuix the kirk and the twa Flemyng wobsters," they were to end their work between the date of the entry (8th May) and 1st September next to come, and in the meantime to confer with the ministers "anes at the leist ilk owlk in the ile of the kirk"; and if they did not make their peace with the Kirk they were to depart the realm on the date named. The town of Edinburgh paid them £68 6s. 8d. for their travelling expenses, which was afterwards repaid the burgh by the Laird of Dairsie and Mr. Arch. Wilkin, and finally given to the Trinity Kirk for making repairs on it.

The Convention of Royal Burghs recommended in 1570 that the exportation of wool outwith the realm should be forbidden by an Act of Parliament, but in 1578 the same body determined that no impediment should be put in the way of those who export to Norway "schone,[27] salt, malt, or linen cloth," in order that they might bring back timber. The desire to restrain any foreign traffic in wool was a very strong point at this period with the mercantile interest in Scotland. The Convention at Linlithgow made an Act prohibiting the export of wool under a penalty of 500 merks. James Fleming, sometime a burgess of Perth, was reported to the Convention of Royal Burghs as "amassing in sundry pairts of the realme ane intolerable quantity of wool" to transport to Flanders, and all magistrates were commanded to prevent ships carrying it. It is evident, however, that this policy was not unanimous. In 1600 the city of Edinburgh, being accused of slackness in the matter of restraining the export of wool, produced to the Convention an instrument "be awyse of men of men of law" showing that this policy would be eventually very prejudicial to the burghs, but the burghs would not be persuaded and persisted in their action. However, the Privy Council, on the 5th of February, 1600, took the matter up and annulled and discharged the pretended Act as a usurpation of the Royal authority, and gave free license to all merchants to export wool and linen cloth and to import all sorts of English cloth, up to the 1st December following. The Scottish Parliament provided by an Act in 1601 that unless the burghs availed themselves of the privileges formerly granted to them for the manufacture of textiles before the next term of Michaelmas they should lose the immunities promised, and the King should then have the right of granting such to anyone.

At an extraordinary sederunt of the Privy Council on the 24th of July the Bailies of Edinburgh appeared to answer to a charge made against them by the strangers lately brought into the country from Flanders for improving the cloth manufacture that they were neither "intertaneit nor putt to the werk," and " that they were sinderit,[28] quhilk wald be a grit hinder to the perfectioun of the said werk," and the Bailies were ordered to keep them together in Edinburgh, notwithstanding any ordinance set down by the Commissioners of burghs anent separating the strangers and planting them severally in other towns. And until they were set to work Edinburgh was to provide them with meat and drink and to be proportionately relieved by the other burghs. Another Act of the Estates in February, 1601, is referred to in the minute of 14th February of the Convention of Burghs, but it is not to be found in the Record Edition. Apparently it provided that twenty more craftsmen, "makeris of claith and lauboureris of woll" should be brought from abroad, and the burghs accordingly agreed to uplift 12,000 merks towards the expense. On the 2nd of June the Privy Council demanded a definite answer from the Convention, to be given not later than the 9th of July, as to when they would be prepared to set up cloth making. Accordingly, the Convention, having directed commissioners to proceed to France, Flanders, and England on the 30th of July, heard a report from Andrew Hunter, who had gone to Norwich, that he had hopes of agreeing with one Gabriel Bischop, clothmaker there, to come to Scotland, and also from Thomas Fischer, who had gone to France, that he had not been successful. A committee was appointed to make a final arrangement, and they had, on the 10th of July, a long conference with Bischop, and agreed with him to come to Edinburgh and set up a cloth manufactory there. Hunter had also procured the services of certain Dutch weavers from Leyden, and they were divided amongst the other burghs. Ayr took three of them —George Baert, " plotter "[29] and camber "[30]; James Claers, weaver; and Arane Janson, " scherar."[31] Perth received Jacque de la Rudge, " camber and spyner "[32]; Jacob Petersen, " scherar"; and Abigail Vanhort, " spyner woman"; and Claus Losseir, Cornelius Dermis, and Henre de Turk went to Dundee. The same day the Commissioners approved of the following articles being laid before

Privy Council :—(First) that the burghs should have power to put in force the Acts against the export of wool ; (second) that no duty should be imposed on cloth not transported out of the country ; (third) that the magistrates of each burgh, and they only, should have the control of the cloth made in the burgh ; and (fourth) that Andrew Hunter should not be troubled on account of his liabilities as sole cautioner for Thomas Foulis and Robert Jousy.

A difference of opinion still existed between the King and the burghs as to the best method of utilizing the services of the strangers. The King accordingly addressed a letter to the Convention urging the Commissioners further to consider the matter, but it does not appear what the result was.

From a minute of the Convention of Burghs on the 2nd of February, 1605, it would appear that an Act of Parliament had been passed on the 7th of June giving an offer to the burghs to work the cloth factories, though no mention is made of it in the Record Edition of the Acts. The burghs declined the offer on the double ground that they had no more interest in cloth manufacture than any other part of the realm, and that they had sustained great losses by the former attempts to set it up ; but they agreed to give their "fortefecatioun and concurrence" to anyone who would undertake the work.

The next notice to be found of these foreigners is

in 1609, when they were established in the Canongate of Edinburgh, and were being still molested by the magistrates; but, on appeal to the Privy Council, they were exempted from their interference. During the remainder of the reign of James VI., who consistently and perseveringly took every opportunity of promoting and improving native manufactures, considerable progress seems to have been made in the woollen industries. In 1613 Scottish cloth, plaiding, and kerseys [33] were exported to the Low Countries, showing that home wants were not only fully supplied, but a surplus left for foreign trade.

One of the first Acts of Charles I. in 1625 was strongly to recommend the burghs of Scotland still to continue establishing manufactories, and the same advice was repeated in 1633. A further step was taken in 1641, when a Royal Executive Commission was created by Act of Parliament, specially for the purpose of encouraging Scottish industries. After reciting the various measures formerly taken for the same purpose, and specially referring to the Acts of Parliament of 1581 and 1597; of Privy Council of May, 1597; July, 1600; November, 1601; December, 1601; May, 1612; October, 1614; August, 1616; July, 1620; February, 1623; July, 1623, and the Acts of Convention of June, 1605; November, 1625; and August, 1626, the Act declares that in spite of all that had been done no considerable progress had been made " for want of cherishing, interteenement, and right order of prosecutione thereof"; and accordingly gives and grants to certain persons to be nominated by the Privy Council full powers to give every encouragement to all sorts of manufactories within the kingdom. These powers of the Commissioners were very wide indeed. They could summon before them anyone who could give any information; they could make rules and fix wages; and could compel idle and dissolute persons either to work or go to the houses of correction, which were to be erected if need be. They could also make corporations, and grant to them all the privileges formerly conferred. It was further declared that all Spanish wool and other necessaries required for the works should be imported duty free; and that the manufactured products should be free from custom for fifteen years. The workmen were to be exempted from all taxation, and were not to be interfered with by anyone. In the Minutes of Parliament of 8th September, 1641, a very important overture was considered, and ordered to be given in to the Estates to be advised upon. After reciting that the want of manufactories within the kingdom occasioned great poverty and loss, inasmuch as fifteen hundred thousand pounds (Scots) were sent out of the country yearly to buy foreign manufactured goods, and caused besides various other evils, it was desired that in every shire a school should be erected in one or other of the burghs, at the expense of the burgh, and that every parish within the shire should send either one or two boys, according to the valuation of the parish, to be taught for seven years all sort of "working cloth, or seys,[34] spinning, weaving, waaking, litting, and dressing." Towards the expense of maintaining and teaching the boys an assessment of a merk from every chalder victual, or 100 merks of valued rent was to be paid, one-half by the owners, the other half by the occupiers. Every boy was to be above ten years of age. This is probably the earliest attempt at systematic technical teaching in Scotland.

In 1645 the privileges of manufacturers and their workmen in being exempt from all military service and public taxation were again ratified. In March, 1655, the Protector gave instructions to his Council in Scotland to advance manufactories by every means in their power, and to advise and report thereanent.

For a very long time (tradition says for several centuries) Haddington had been the seat of a woollen manufactory, established in a suburb called the Nungate. During Cromwell's time an English company, of which a Colonel Stansfield was the principal partner, expended a large sum of money in purchasing lands formerly belonging to the monastery of Haddington, and erecting mills and machinery, at a place called New Mills. After the restoration Colonel Stansfield was knighted, and in 1687 he was barbarously murdered by his eldest son. The trial was a very curious one, on account of the stress laid by the King's Advocate when prosecuting on the fact that the corpse of Sir Philip Stansfield had bled when touched by the murderer.

About this time other woollen factories were established at Bonnington, near Edinburgh, at Ayr, and, in 1681, at Glasgow, by James Armour, who had an Act of Parliament in his favour permitting him to import his raw material free of duty, allowing his products to be untaxed for nineteen years, and granting his workers the usual exemptions from watching, warding, and militia service. This was not, however, the earliest attempt to establish woollen manufactories in Glasgow. In 1648 the burgh appointed John Johnstone to "speir[35] out" men fitting to be employed, and to report. Next year a bargain was made with James Bell to sell his "work loomes" and make over his interest in the work to the town; and in 1650 "ane Inglis clothiar," apparently one Simon Pitchersgill, was put in charge of the work at a salary of £45. Probably the venture was not very successful, for in 1652 it was intimated by "touk[36] of drume" that the factory would be let to the highest bidder, and accordingly a new tack was granted to James Hamilton, Thomas Allan, and John Neill.

The old tenant, however, got it again in 1653, and in 1660 it was let to the weavers for seven years, at an annual rent of £60.

During the years 1661-1673 several Acts of Parliament came into force with the object of still further stimulating and encouraging native industries. The raw materials of all manufactures were freed from custom. The former Acts were confirmed and extended. In each parish competent persons were to be appointed to teach the poorer children to fine and spin wool and to knit stockings. An impost of 20 per cent. was laid on various commodities, such as ribbons, thread, etc., on the manufacturers first finding caution to produce an article as good and as cheap as that imported, and to employ native apprentices. All these privileges and encouragements were once more confirmed and granted by another Act in 1681, and in the same year the weavers of Glasgow were incorporated. Through the exertions of the Duke of York, a body of merchants were associated for the purpose of setting up another textile factory at New Mills. The work made a modest commencement with two looms, but soon extended to twenty-five, and was incorporated by Act of Parliament in 1693. Up to this year the production had not been extensive, for in 1683 General Dalyell and Graham of Claverhouse had to import cloth from England for their troops. The army clothing was obtained from that country, though the New Mills Company offered to make it as cheaply and of as good quality. But after the Act of 1693 Parliament ordered all the woollen cloth required for the army to be of home manufacture. After that the company seem to have prospered, and came very frequently under the notice of Parliament. They were exempted from supply in 1695; they obtained an Act against foreign importation in 1696; another special Act in their favour was prepared in 1700, and they were exempted specially from taxation in the years 1704, 1705, and 1706.

From this period down to the Union the woollen industry made considerable progress. Factories were started in 1701 at Musselburgh, Glasgow, and near Edinburgh. Shortly afterwards we find them at North Mills, Aberdeen, and elsewhere.

CHAPTER IV.

MANUFACTURES.

TURNING now to the linen manufacture, we find, from the "Assisa de Tolloneis," that, at the time of Bruce, the custom on every 100 lb. of linen was one halfpenny. No further notice of it is found in the public records till 1573, when an Act of Parliament was passed forbidding it to be exported. It seems to have continued to make progress, and in the Parliament of 1639 another Act was passed to encourage this rising industry. After reciting that linen had now become "ane of the pryme commodities of this kingdome, wherby many people are put to worke and money is brought within the same, which, pairtly throughe the deceet used by the bleicheres in lymeing thereof and pairtlie by the uncertaintie of the breadth, is lyklie to come in contempt abroade, to the great prejudice of this kingdome," therefore it was forbidden for anyone to make or sell linen cloth of less breadth than one ell if the price per ell was ten shillings or above, or of less breadth than three-quarters of an ell if the price was under ten shillings. Bleaching with lime was forbidden under heavy penalties, and all linen was to be presented in the market by the "selvedge and not by the rige."

That the manufacture had made some progress is shown by the imposition in 1661 of two ounces of bullion for each 100 ells exported, and in the same year another Act was passed to encourage the establishment of companies and societies for making linen cloth stuffs. This Act provided that no stuffs should be exported except made by such a society; that all their raw material should be free of duty for 19 years; that they might make regulations for their trade; and that all vagabonds, idlers, and poor children were to be instructed to fine and mix wool, spin worsted, and knit stockings.

The Act to encourage trade and manufactures, which was passed in 1681, lays down with great minuteness the conditions of textile manufactures at this period in Scotland. The provision as to the breadth of cloth given in former Acts was repeated. All linen was to be made up in pieces and half pieces, the pieces to contain 24 ells. Druggets, fingram, and plaiding were to be of the breadth of ¾ and one nail. Serges were to be 50 or 52 ells in the piece, with a breadth of 1 ell and 2 inches. They were not to be stretched in the rolling, and were to be made up in folds 1 ell or ¾ long.

An extraordinary regulation was made by the Scottish Parliament in 1686. It was declared to be a punishable offence for any person to be buried except in linen dead clothes made in Scotland, under a penalty of £200 or £300 if a nobleman. This regulation actually remained in force till 1707.

A curious transaction took place in 1691. The Convention of Royal Burghs on the 20th October desired their thanks to be conveyed to the Earl of Melville and the Master of Stair for "putting a stop to a new project of erecting a linen manufacture within the kingdom." This "new project" was that some Englishmen should set up a linen manufactory which would interfere with the home trade. Accordingly the burghs petitioned the Privy Council to put the laws anent the manufacture in force, and ordered a present of 2,000 merks to be sent to the two Secretaries of State "for their good services done," and £50 as a gratuity to the Under-Secretary for his trouble. From an entry in the minutes of Convention in 1694 it would appear, however, that the English company did set up their factory after all.

Further regulations were made in 1693, and the same year a manufactory was established in the citadel of Leith with all the privileges accorded by the laws, for the space of 21 years. They had very arbitrary powers over their workmen, and could retain them until they served out their time. They had also a seal granted them to seal all their stuff with, and their privileges extended to their bleaching fields at Bonington, and later (1695) to Corstorphine. They could make laws and regulations and appoint a bailie to hold courts for the punishment of offences committed by their workmen. The workmen and others could claim exemption from certain public burdens, such as billeting of soldiers, and moreover, did not require to pay excise duties for any liquors consumed by themselves.

In 1700 John Corse, of Glasgow, petitioned that he might be allowed to have a linen manufactory with all the privileges. Further Acts of Parliament for measuring and sealing linen were passed 1700, 1701, and 1703. The merchants of Edinburgh petitioned against the wearing of linen in 1705 on the ground that it interfered with the woollen manufacturers.

Of the silk textiles we have very scanty traces in early Scottish history. In the time of David I. hucksters were forbidden to buy silk except in fair time. On account of the poverty of the kingdom, and the expense of importing silk, it was forbidden in 1471 to be worn except by knights, ministers, heralds, and persons worth £100 per annum of rent. A Commission was appointed in 1579 to inquire anent the art of silk manufacture. The result of this was the establishment in Perth, in 1581, of a considerable silk manufactory by a Robert Dickson. Privilege was given him by Parliament to set agoing a manufactory, and to bring into the realm and teach the art of making and working silk as good as that of France or Flanders, and to sell it cheaper. The raw material required, and the drugs for dyeing the fabric, were to be imported by him free of duty, and the products of his factory were to be also untaxed. He and his workmen, to the number of 100, were to be exempt from all burdens, taxation, and impositions. And these privileges were to last for 30 years. There is no trace of any other silk manufactory till 1697, when two merchants, by name Ormeston and Elliot, obtained a grant from the Privy Council to enable them to establish a manufactory for the purpose of winding, throwing, twisting, and dyeing silk.

In 1703 a petition from the silk manufacturers was presented to the Parliament of Scotland, but the consideration of it was delayed until the condition of the whole manufacture could be considered.

We do not propose to carry the history of textile manufactures at this time later than the Union; but it is curious to compare the dismal prophecies that were then made of the inevitable decline of Scottish trade and commerce which was supposed to be the certain results of that measure with the actual facts of history. When the Act of Union was under the consideration of the Scottish Parliament, the then Lord Belhaven made a famous speech which produced a great impression on the country, and which is still preserved in the libraries of the curious. Speaking in a vein of prophecy, always a dangerous line for a practical politician, he says, referring to the commercial and manufacturing interests of the towns :—

"My Lord Chancellor,—When I consider this affair of an union betwixt the two nations, as it is expressed in the several articles thereof, and now the subject of our deliberation at this time, I find my mind crowded with a variety of very melancholy thoughts. . . . I think I see the royal state of burghs walking their desolate streets, hanging down their heads under disappointments; wormed out of all the branches of their old trade, uncertain what hand to turn to, necessitated to become 'prentices to their unkind neighbours, and yet, after all, finding their trade so fortified by companies and secured by prescriptions that they despair of any success therein. . . . I think I see the honest, industrious tradesman loaded with new taxes and impositions, disappointed of the equivalents, drinking water in place of ale, and eating saltless porridge."

It is perhaps fortunate that though we are permitted to prophesy, we are denied the power of bringing our prophecies to pass.

Having treated of the early textile manufactures of Scotland, we come now to the other branches. And probably one of the earliest was that of salt. In the reign of David I. salt works became objects of great attention, and constant reference is made to them in the Chartularies. That King granted to the monks of Kelso a salt work on the northern shore of the Forth, and to the monks of Newbattle one at "Blackeland," and another at "Calentyr." From the same King the Abbey of Cambuskenneth got a salt pan, the monks of Holyrood a salt pan and twenty-six acres of land at Airth, and the monks of Jedburgh a salt work at Stirling. William the Lion was the owner of several salt works, and bestowed one on the Abbey of Aberbrothock. Roland of Galloway gave the monks of Kelso a salt work on the Solway, with liberty to take wood from his forests for the pans. Duncan of Carrick made a similar gift to the Abbey of Melrose from his lands of Turnberry, in Ayrshire, and the same convent had other salt pans near Ayr from Roger de Scalebroc. In 1536 the price of salt was to be fixed by Royal Commissioners along with the Provost of Edinburgh; and the Magistrates in all coast towns were empowered to settle at what rate imported salt was to be sold at. Various improvements were introduced into the manufacture shortly afterwards. In 1563 an Act of Parliament prohibited anyone from making salt after the new method introduced by certain strangers without special license for fifty years. No salt could be exported from any salt work without a written license, only granted on proof that six bolls weekly from each pan had been reserved for home consumption. At this period considerable quantities of this article were imported from Spain and Brittany, but in 1587 Lady Burleigh was granted for seven years the privilege of making refined salt for salting salmon and other fish which could not be salted with "small salt," and thus the necessity for using the foreign commodity was obviated. Further improvements were introduced by Eustacius Roche, a Fleming, and in consideration thereof he received in 1599 a monopoly of the manufacture of "great salt." In 1640 an Act was passed prohibiting Sunday work in the salt pans, which was confirmed in 1661.

A curious account of this industry is given in the report made to the Government of the Protector as to the excise and customs in Scotland in 1656. From that account we gather that the northern parts of Scotland were then chiefly served with foreign salt from France, and the western with English salt; and that the chief native supply came from the salt pans between St. Andrews and Stirling on the one side of the Forth, and between Stirling and Berwick on the other. The proprietors of these pans were usually called "masters," and the workers "makers." The latter received no wages, but contracted to supply the masters with a certain amount of salt per pan, and the overplus they kept for themselves. The masters provided all the coals, and stored their proportion of the salt in "garnels"[37] for exportation chiefly to England or beyond the seas. The makers sold their proportion to cadgers, who hawked it about the country in creels on horseback for home consumption. Tucker, who makes the report, gives a very poor account of the workmen or makers. He says that "besides their infinite povertye and miserableness they are to be esteemed rather brutes than rationals"; and in another place speaks of their "vilenesse" and "unworthinesse." The whole amount of custom paid on home-made salt in the year 1656 was only £810. In 1661 Colonel Ludovic Leslie and Colonel James Scott obtained a monopoly of the manufacture for twelve years, and in 1681 all the salt works in Scotland were declared to be public manufactories, and to be entitled to all the privileges thereof. Robert Cuninghame, of Auchinbarvie, had a grant in 1686, confirmed and extended in 1693, for the purpose of making a harbour at Saltcoats, on the Ayrshire coast, for the better exportation of the coal and salt "wherewith that country abounds." Sir John Shaw, of Greenock, introduced a new method of making salt, and in consequence the privileges of a manufactory were extended to him and his partners in 1696. Other improvements were made by Mr. William Erskine, who got similar privileges; and later on by Mr. George Campbell, a merchant in Edinburgh. Salt occupied a considerable share of attention during the negotiations for the Union in 1706, and the Duke of Athole protested against any duty being laid on it by the contemplated measure.

Of the early fictile industries in Scotland our knowledge is very limited. Rude pottery was undoubtedly made in considerable quantities even in the prehistoric ages, and before the use of the wheel was known. Occasionally specimens of a later period have been discovered, but there is no evidence of any extensive manufacture until comparatively modern times. "Duo godecta vytrea" are recorded in 1291 as being contained in a chest in the dormitory at Holyrood, but they may have been of foreign origin.

In 1690 Sir George Hay of Nethercliff had the gift of a license to make glass and iron in Scotland for thirty-one years, which was confirmed by the Scotch Parliament in 1612. His work was established at Wemyss in Fife. "Braid" glass, or window glass, was made equal in quality to best Danskine; but bottles and other ware not being of sufficient excellence, some specimens were brought from England and deposited in Edinburgh Castle to serve as patterns in point of quality. In 1621 the Privy Council granted Hay a monopoly of the manufacture, but restricted the price to twelve pounds the "cradle" or case. A tax of 5 per cent. on the value was put on glass in 1655; and a little later an ounce of bullion was to be brought to the Mint for every twelve dozen of drinking glasses and glass bottles exported. James Turner, a cabinetmaker in Edinburgh, "having with much labour, pains, and expenses, attained to the skill and art of making of cabinets, mirror glasses, and the like curious work," the Deacon and Incorporation of the Wrights of Edinburgh interrupted his factory, seized on his tools, and fined him £20 sterling; but the Privy Council in 1678 and in 1685, and Parliament in 1695, decreed that he should have full liberty to exercise his work and trade without molestation from anyone. Another glass manufactory was set up at Leith, to which in 1689 the Privy Council granted the privileges of a manufactory, and prohibited the introduction of foreign bottles into the country, only providing that the Leith work should not charge more than two and sixpence the dozen. In 1698 the manufactory at Wemyss seems to have passed into the hands of Lord Elcho, who received an Act of Parliament confirming the grant of the privileges of a manufactory formerly made by the Privy Council, and giving him a monopoly for nine years of certain new kinds of glass never before made in Scotland (viz., coach glasses and moulded glasses) unless some other manufactory was started within two years. It was specially provided that this grant was not to prejudice the privileges formerly given to the manufactory at Leith or to that at Aitchison's Haven, which was established by William Morison, of Preston Grange, in 1697, for the making of all sorts of glass, "as bottles, vials, drinking, window, mirror, and warck glasses." Among the foreigners who were engaged at Morison's work was a Frenchman, Leblanc, who was skilled in the art of polishing glass, an art never hitherto practised in Scotland. The first glass work in Glasgow was started in 1701 by James Montgomery, who applied to the Privy Council for a license to make bottles to supply the West Country, seeing that the transit of such breakable goods from Leith and Morison's Haven was attended with vast charge and great hazard. He proposed to use wood ashes and fern ash, of which there was great abundance in the West Country, to make, first, good white soap, and the rest into glass. The Privy Council granted his request accordingly. Robert Douglas, Leith, had a manufactory of porcelain and earthenware there in 1695, and in 1703 an Act was passed in favour of William Montgomery, of Macbiehill, and George Linn, merchant in Edinburgh, who set up "a pot-house with kills, mills, warehouse, and other conveniences for making Lame,[38] Purslane, and Earthen Ware," and had brought competent persons from abroad to teach the natives the proper mode of manufacture, giving them not only the ordinary privileges of a manufactory, but a monopoly for fifteen years.

Soap was not an article manufactured in Scotland at a very early period. What was used seems to have been imported apparently from the Low Countries. It is mentioned as part of the "*conveth*" of the Abbey of Scone in 1164, and the custom payable on each "kyste or schryno[39] of sapo," as given in the Assisa de Tolloneis was twopence. In 1619 a privilege was granted to Nathaniel Uddart to make soap at his works in Leith, and in 1621 the Privy Council prohibited the importation of foreign soap, but fixed the maximum price of the native manufacture at £24 per barrel (of 16 stones) for green soap, and £32 per same barrel of white soap. This grant was, however, very unpopular, and in consequence of the numerous complaints made about it, the prohibition against foreign importation was threatened to be withdrawn unless a better article was provided at a cheaper rate. This patent lasted twenty-one years, and at its expiration another was granted to Patrick Maule, of Panmure, " His Majesty's daily servitor," for thirty-one years at a yearly rental of £20 sterling. He had at the same time a license to fish and trade in the country and seas of Greenland for materials necessary for his work. In 1695 an Act of Parliament was passed in favour of Robert Douglas (who is described in it as "a great promoter of manufactories" for many years, and is apparently the same individual formerly mentioned), to enable him to get the privileges granted to manufactories for his soap work at Leith, which "had much contributed to setting up the trade with Archangel and Russia," and these privileges were accordingly granted to him for nineteen years. A petition was presented in 1700 by the same James Montgomery, who erected the glass works in Glasgow, to have the privileges of a manufactory extended to his soap work there.

The manufacture of paper can claim a fairly early origin in Scotland. In 1590, Peter Groot Heare, a German, along with some partners, received a license from the Privy Council to establish a paper work, with all the privileges belonging to a manufactory, for nine years after the 1st of August next. In 1675, another work was set up at Dalry Mills, near Edinburgh, but very soon after it was burnt down. However, in 1679, it was going on and producing gray and blue paper of a better quality than had ever been made before in this country. French workmen were employed, but many Scots were instructed in the trade. The proprietors were impeded in their operations by a "faulty custom" in the country of using good rags to make candlewicks. They accordingly petitioned the Privy Council to prohibit rags being used for this purpose, which they did. No further notice of this work occurs in the public records, but it was probably not successful, for in 1693 Nicolas Dupin petitioned the Privy Council for permission to set up a paper manufactory. He was supported in his enterprise by some Scotchmen in London, who told him that there was no good writing paper to be got in Scotland, those who had already attempted the manufacture having failed. He claimed to be able to make all sorts of fine paper as good or better than any made beyond seas, and far cheaper; and he proposed, besides, to bring in some "ingenious outlandish workmen" to teach their art in the kingdom. All his paper was to have the arms of Scotland as the water mark; and the company were granted the same power over their instructed workmen as the cloth factory at Newmilns had. This company had an Act of the Scotch Parliament passed in its favour in 1695. The Act having recited that "it being found that the water and air in several parts of this kingdom are very fitt and may contribut much to the success of such a work," empowered Dupin and Denis Manes and their partners to be incorporated by the name of "the Scots White Paper Manufactory," with all the privileges and immunities contained in the Acts for encouraging commercial undertakings.

Sugar came into use in Scotland at a comparatively late period. There was a tax put on it in 1655, which shows it must have been known commonly before that time. In 1681 two sugar works at Glasgow were declared to be manufactories under the provisions of the Acts for encouraging manufactures. These works belonged to Frederick Hamilton and John Corse and other partners, who had an Act of Parliament in their favour, allowing them, in addition to the usual immunities, to grant " transires " without applying to the Custom House. Another work was in operation in Leith in 1695, and had the same privileges which were granted to Glasgow, including that of making 18 tons of rum yearly free of duty. Hugh and James Montgomerie, merchants in Glasgow, had an Act of Incorporation in 1696 for the purpose of starting another sugar work in Glasgow (called "a suggarie") under the style and title of " The New Sugar Manufactory of Glasgow," with all the privileges of law, to endure for nineteen years. Another sugar work was started in Glasgow by Matthew and Daniel Campbell in

1700, who also proposed to the Privy Council to distil brandy and other strong waters.

In 1686 the Estates of the Realm, " takeing to consideration the great advantage that the nation may have by the trade of founding lately brought in to this kingdom by John Meikle for casting of bells, cannons, and *other such useful instruments*," granted him the rights, privileges, and immunities under the Acts of 1661 and 1681.

Cannons would not be of much use without gunpowder, so we find that four years later Mr. James Gordon applied for a license to make that commodity. Gordon was a merchant of London, as his memorial sets forth, "who, by the blessing of God has acquired the most necessary skill of making of salt peter and Gunpowder," and desired "for the generall benefite of his native Countrey . . . to prosecute the said good and beneficiall designe." An Act was prepared and is recorded in 1690 (though it is doubtful whether it ever passed), granting the necessary permission, prohibiting any one from importing gunpowder, and providing that every barrel of the native manufacture should be sealed with a seal to be provided by Gordon. He was also empowered "to cause take up the bottoms of floors, cellars, vaults, and other out houses such as doucats,[40] old castells, Towers, fortalices, churches, chappells, creeks, pitts and coaves, &c., in any place within the kingdome where peterish earth shall be found, and to dispose thereof for the convenience of the gunpowder manufactories."

The first notice we have in the public records respecting gunpowder is in 1535, when the merchants were ordained to import it. Some time previous to 1630 a patent had been granted for its manufacture in Scotland, for in that year Parliament was petitioned "that the persoun to whome the gift was givin may ather convenientlie and tymouslie take vpon him the dew performance or otherwayes that his patent be recalled." The Earl of Linlithgow was probably the person meant, as, when monopolies were abolished in 1641, he was recompensed for the outlay he had incurred on his powder-works. Another gunpowder-work was established in 1695 by Sir Alexander Hope of Kerse and others.

In 1693 Parliament, taking into consideration the great loss and inconvenience sustained by the lieges by reason of the want of tradesmen for making coaches, chariots, sedans, coach-harness, and other fittings, empowered William Scott, cabinetmaker, to set up a manufactory for the same, with all the privileges belonging to it. James Lyell of Gairden had "applyed himselfe for these many yeares for improving of lint, hemp, and rape seeds for the making of good oyl out of the grains within this kingdom," and an Act in his favour was passed in Parliament in 1695. He also set up a manufactory "of rabbet and hair skins . . . by bringing them first into wooll and then into hatts, which is now exported, and then returned in fforeign hatts." Another oil work was established in 1700 by James Turner, but no further notice of it occurs in the public records.

The rapid rise and continual growth of Scottish manufactures after the Union belongs to a later period of history, and does not come within the scope of the present design. But enough has been given to show the keen and anxious desire to encourage manufacturing industries which prevailed in this country for more than two centuries before the desired result was actually achieved.

CHAPTER V.

FISHERIES.

OF old the Scottish Fisheries occupied an important position among the national industries. The fishing for salmon belonged to the Crown, and could not be enjoyed by any subject without a special grant by charter, though a right of salmon fishing followed a general grant of fishing after forty years prescription. David I. gave to the Abbey of Holyrood a right to have one draw of a net for salmon, and in 1164 the Abbey of Scone had two nets in the Tay, one at "Kyncarrekyn," and the other at the *"insula regis"*; and one net in the Forth at Stirling. By a law of the time of William I., the midstreams of all salmon rivers were to be free for the length of a three-year-old pig, rather a curious standard of measurement. In the time of Alexander III. salmon might be fished in all waters except those flowing into the sea. No one could fish for salmon anywhere from Saturday night till sunrise on Monday; nor in "forbidden time," under the "old penalty." Offenders against the salmon fishery laws were liable to forty days' imprisonment, and anyone thrice convicted suffered death. It was also forbidden to catch salmon in nets at mill dams, salmon fry at lades or dams, and "red fish" at any time. Unseasonable fish ("salmones corrupti"), if offered for sale, were to be seized and sent to the lepers, or destroyed. The close time in all rivers was between the Feast of the Assumption of the Virgin (15th August), and Martinmas. Young salmon ("salmunculi") could not be legally taken between the middle of April, and the Feast of St. John the Baptist (24th June).

Occasionally, however, special exceptions were made. Thus, Olifaunt of Gask had permission to fish the water of Erne three days a week during the close time. But in 1424 it was enacted that all persons infeft in the privilege of fishing in close time were to abstain for three years. Many enactments were made from this period down to the Union, dealing with taking fish in close time. In 1489 the clear space in midstream to be left for the salmon to get up, was ordered to be five feet. In 1632 fishing smacks ("bushes") were forbidden to approach within fourteen miles of the coast between Redhead and Buchan Ness, so as not to interfere with the salmon fishing in the rivers. An extraordinary proposal was submitted to Parliament in 1645 by Hugo L'Amey, a Frenchman. It involved a Scots colony in the Indies; a great trade with the same country; the annual building of three "great shippes" of four hundred tons a-piece, and three "pinnaces" of fifty tons a-piece, and of which, when thirty-six were built, twelve might be employed in the defence of the Scottish coasts, and merchant adventures on the high seas, and twenty-four in the Indian trade; and all without any tax or imposition whatever, but to be paid for out of the increased value of the salmon fishings. M. L'Amey only asked that the salmon and other fishing in Scotland should be "accommodat and made up for the sale at his appointment." Besides the public and national advantages, M. L'Amey promised the proprietors of the salmon fishings one third higher price than ever they had had before, and the merchant traders thirty per cent. more profits. To relieve the great burden of poverty in the country, the Frenchman further proposed to plant Indian wheat in Scotland, which would yield fourfold more meal, and not impoverish the ground. The proposal was remitted to a committee, but no further trace of it is found in the Parliamentary Records.

Towards the close of the 17th century, the close time for the Dee, Don, Spey, Findhorn, Ythan,

Conon, Bewlie, Ness, and Deveron was from 8th September to 1st January, and in the Nith from 1st March to 1st November.

Trout are mentioned in the Act of 1469, prohibiting for three years the use of " coups,"[41] narrow mesh nets, and "prins"[42] in rivers running into the sea; and another statute of 1633 forbids any fish to be killed in burns falling into the Loch of Leven, within five miles of it, in order to preserve the "pykes, perches, and trouts" of that famous fishing water.

Anyone taking pike out of ponds was liable to a fine of £10 Scots by an Act of 1503; and by another in 1535 the offender was ordered to be treated as a thief. The standard measure of salmon barrels in 1573 was twelve gallons of the Stirling pint. The staple markets for the salmon exportation trade were Aberdeen, Elgin, Perth, and Dundee. The standard measure for salmon barrels was kept at Aberdeen, and each burgh had a pattern of it.

The salmon fisheries were a valuable source of revenue to the Crown. In the beginning of the reign of James I. a duty of 2s. 6d. Scots per pound of value was imposed on salmon "bocht be strangers and had out of the realme." In 1426 the custom was imposed on natives as well as foreigners, and, in place of the *ad valorem* duty, the tax was charged on the large or Hamburg barrel (valued at £2), and the small or herring barrel (valued at £1). At this period the average yield of duty from the ports of Aberdeen, Banff, and Montrose was £115, representing a value of £920 worth of salmon exported.

In 1466 the rate of duty was 3s. a barrel, which was raised in 1481 to 4s. Aberdeen claimed an immunity from the higher figure, at anyrate till 1488. Even at the lower figure the revenue from the duty was £135 annually, the largest in Scotland. Berwick produced £44; Banff, £47; Perth, £29; Elgin, £15; Dundee, £14; Montrose, £7; Stirling, £6; and the whole of Scotland, £310.

The sea fisheries were an object of particular attention in Scotland in mediæval times. The Abbey of Holyrood had a grant of the right of fishing for herring from David I. By an Act of Parliament in 1471 certain burghs and lords were bound to provide ships and nets for the sea fishing. Acts of Parliament regulating the fishing and taking of herrings on the west coast were passed in 1487, 1496, and 1579. The staple ports for the herring and white fish trade were, in 1584, Leith, Crail, Ayr, and Dumbarton.

A duty of one penny was imposed in 1424 on every thousand fresh herring sold within the country; four shillings were charged for each last of twelve barrels barrelled by Scotsmen; six shillings if barrelled by strangers; and fourpence for every thousand red herring. The amount of money raised from the custom of Loch Fyne herrings was returned by the custumars of Irvine at £10 in 1479; £17 in 1480; and £34 in 1481. The custumars of Dumbarton returned £170 from the same source about the same period, and in 1487 the revenue derived from the custom on herrings from the "Lows" (*i.e.*, the Clyde lochs, not the island of the Lews) at the high figure of £379. The herring barrels were each to contain nine gallons of the Stirling pint; and were ordered in 1540 when of the standard size to be marked with the cooper's iron and that of the town.

A very curious document about the Scotch herring fishing is preserved in the Acts of the Parliaments of Scotland. In 1630 Charles I. made certain proposals to the Privy Council in Scotland anent a scheme for a general fishing. Besides employing existing fishing boats, it was proposed to build 200 new vessels of from 30 to 50 tons burden each. The cost of the hull and iron work was estimated at £3 per ton. The same rate was estimated for rigging, sails, cables, anchors, masts, boats, etc. One hundred and twenty nets were to be provided for each ship, with head lines and corks, at one pound for each fitted net. Two hundred and fifty fathoms of rope were allowed to each ship, at a cost of £16 13s. 4d., and other necessaries were estimated at £4 per ship. Thus the total cost of each fishing vessel, taking 40 tons burden as the average, would be £386 13s. 4d. Each boat was to make three fishing expeditions per annum. The first was to be for herrings, and the catch was estimated at 100 last, or 1,200 barrels of fish. To cure these would take £120 worth of salt, at the then prices. The crew of each average sized ship consisted of 16 men and boys, who cost for victuals 13s. 4d. a month each, with a money wage of £74 per crew for the four months of the herring fishing.

As against this expenditure the profit of the three fishings was estimated as follows. The first fishing of the 200 vessels was to produce 20,000 last of herrings, and each last sold at sea was to bring in £10; the second fishing (October to February) was to produce 12,000 last at £12; and the third fishing (ling and cod), from March till June, was estimated to produce 1,200,000 fish, at £30 the 1,000, besides the worth of the oil.

This fleet was to be worked principally from the Lews for the western coasts, and the King proposed to annex that island to the Crown, making proper satisfaction to the Earl of Seaforth, and to establish in it certain free burghs for fishing purposes.

In connection with this Fishery Company an interesting notice is found regarding the territorial waters of Scotland. ·Considerable jealousy was apparently felt by the Scotch Privy Council that the fishing rights of the natives might be interfered with by the proposed new Fishery Company. Accordingly they referred the matter to certain Commissioners to determine the exclusive fishery limits of the Scottish Coast. The Commissioners reported, on the 21st April, 1631, that no Englishmen, nor other foreigners, had ever been allowed to fish within the lochs, bays, and firths, nor within fourteen miles of the coast, and they fixed the exclusive limits, commencing with a straight line drawn from St. Abb's Head to the Red Head, and 14 miles beyond it, then along at the same distance from the coast to Buchan Ness, thence the same distance beyond a straight line drawn to Duncansbay Head; from that point at the same distance round the Orkneys and Shetland to Holburn Head in Caithness, and from the Stour of Assynt to the Butt of Lews, from thence, at the same distance round the western coast of the Long Island, and from thence by a straight line from Barra Head, by the Mull of Ooa in Islay, to the Mull of Kintyre, and from that point up the centre of the Solway to the Scottish March.

These limits were finally somewhat altered; but, on the dissolution of the Fishery Company in 1690, the full rights of the native fishermen were restored by Act of Parliament.

The charter of the General Fishery Company was granted in 1632, and is still preserved.

The society was to be governed by twelve councillors, of whom one-half were to be Scots and the other half English or Irish. The six Scots named were the Earls of Morton, Strathearn, and Roxburgh, Viscount Stirling, John Hay, and George Fletcher. A long list of names were enrolled as members of the society, and extensive powers of jurisdiction were conferred. They were to hold courts, and to have tolbooths in the various districts; and in each district four judges, two of whom were to be Scots, were to be chosen by the council to decide all pleas and cases relating to the fishing trade.

What the success of the company was does not appear from the records; but in 1690 an Act of Parliament was passed dissolving it, and restoring to the lieges their fishing rights, and to the royal burghs their right of export.

In 1661 other statutory facilities were given for the formation and encouragement of societies for herring and white fishing. Each partner was to provide 500 merks Scots of capital, and the companies were to have full power to take fish in all seas, channels, firths, rivers, floods, lakes, and lochs, and to use for fishing purposes all shores, ports, and harbours. With the consent of the Council of Trade, they could appoint certain of their number to make bye-laws for regulating the fishing. They were also privileged to get all their salt, cordage, and other stores free of duty, and to be exempt from all arrestments or citations during the fishing season.

The last Act of any importance relating to the fisheries prior to the Union was passed in 1705. It authorized and empowered all subjects of the Queen within her ancient kingdom of Scotland to take, buy, and cure herring and white fish in all and sundry the seas, bays, etc., of the same. It discharged all Saturday's fishing, top money, stallage,[43] and the like. It enacted that all the barrels should be of the size and quality formerly prescribed; and that fish should be packed, pined,[44] and cured from the bottom to the top with foreign salt only. Every cask was to be marked with the curer's mark as well as the official mark; and all private marks were to be registered in a public register in Edinburgh. The privilege of importing all materials for the fishing industry duty free were confirmed; and the usual penalties for law breakers were continued.

CHAPTER VI.

TAXATION AND REVENUE.

NOT very long ago it would have been practically impossible to write any accurate or consecutive account of the taxation and revenue of the ancient kingdom of Scotland. The earlier chroniclers confined themselves chiefly to recording the historical events of their time, the lives and deaths of the kings, their wars and battles, and the events most nearly concerning the particular districts to which the annalists belonged. The later historians were too busily occupied in inventing an imaginary and purely fabulous account of what the history of Scotland ought, in their opinion, to have been, compounded generally with a total disregard of what, in point of fact, it actually was, to attend to such prosaic matters as those relating to the social or economical condition of their country. But the splendid series of authentic national records which has been already published and is still being issued by the authorities of H.M. General Register House, combined with the important contributions of historical material made by private bodies and individuals, is yearly adding to our knowledge of the past condition of Scotland, and is gradually enabling us to correct the erroneous ideas which have too often and too long hitherto prevailed. The publication of the Acts of the Parliaments of Scotland has placed a mass of reliable facts of the highest importance within the reach of the historical student, the value of which is greatly increased by an elaborate and most valuable index. Second only in importance to this great national record is the Register of the Privy Council, which is now in the course of being issued, while the Rolls of the Exchequer, the Accounts of the Lord High Treasurer, the Register of the Great Seal, and other publications, will, when completed, form a mass of evidence available for future historians which will enable them in many very important points to rewrite the history of Scotland. And the example thus set has been laudably followed by various societies and by public spirited individuals in every part of the country. Perhaps the most important publication after the national records is the Register of the Convention of Royal Burghs, which for all matters relating to one very important subject which will shortly engage our attention, the trade and commerce of early Scotland, is simply invaluable. But the usefulness of this work is greatly marred by the want of an index,[45] thereby causing to the student an intolerable and altogether unnecessary amount of additional labour. It is from the sources above indicated that we derive our only knowledge of the revenues of taxation of Scotland in early times. The fiscal history of Scotland prior to the Union may be conveniently divided into four periods, each possessing different features. The first is characterized by a survival of the earlier Celtic imposts, and extends from a very early period to the reign of David I. The second is marked by feudal services and casualties, and continues till the return of James I. from his captivity in England. The third period closes with the accession of James VI. to the English throne, and exhibits the decay of the feudal principle of aids. The fourth period comes down to the Union, and shows the gradual rise of the modern system of taxes.

It will be necessary to make some preliminary observations. While these characteristics are sufficiently distinct for purposes of division, it is not to be supposed that each period is divided from the other by sharply-defined lines of demarcation. On the contrary, we find in each case the older features and methods gradually becoming extinct, but sometimes surviving for a considerable period in remote parts of the country. It is to be remembered also that a national currency, which now is the familiar medium both of taxation and revenue, was altogether unknown in Scotland prior to the reign of David I. who struck silver pennies; and for a long time afterwards existed only to a very limited amount. Burdens of all sorts, whether private, local, or public, were at first defrayed either by services, or labour, or in kind. We can trace the gradual commutation of these into money payments as the currency extended, and the progress of civilization rendered it more convenient. It is also to be borne in mind that many of the duties and obligations now universally undertaken by the State and paid for by the community by means of taxation were in early times performed directly by individuals. Thus, the duty of national defence was a burden imposed on every free man, and was undertaken by each at his own expense, and it is only in comparatively later times that we find the State gradually incurring charges for military stores, occasionally hiring "wageouris"[46] for particular military services, and so developing into the army estimates of modern days. Similarly, what is now so familiar to us as the Civil Service expenditure had equally modest beginnings. The administration of justice in early times was an unpaid duty which required no national expenditure. Prior to the reign of David I. the expenses of the country and of the sovereign were almost entirely defrayed out of the old prescriptive dues which had descended from the Celtic kingdom, and which were payable by the community to the King, as well as by tenants to their chief. These were the *Cain, Conveth, Feacht,* and *Sluaged* (which we have already noticed as agricultural burdens in the first chapter), with the addition of another called *Ich*, which, Mr. Skene thinks, is probably equivalent to *Ioch*, payment. These are all enumerated in a grant by Sir Ewin of Erregeithill to the Bishop of Argyll in 1251 of lands in Lismore. The *Cain* provided a large revenue in kind, slowly being converted into money with smaller payments in silver, gradually getting larger as the process of commutation extended. The *Conveth*, which originated from the right of the Celtic chiefs not only to be obeyed but to be fed and sustained by the clansmen, appears in the time of Malcolm IV. (in a charter of Scone) to have been a fixed amount of provisions paid in kind. It can be identified with the "*Waytinga,*" a burden laid on the thanages, which, in 1292, was assessed in the Exchequer Rolls at 24 cows per annum for two nights' "waitings" at Forfar, and 13½ cows for a night and a half at Glammis. In Ireland it was called the *Coinmedha*, and was the subsistence of the chief or king when out of his own tilled lands. When systematically due it was called the "Custom of Cuddikie" (*Cuid oidche*), and was restricted to four meals, four times in the year, to the chief and his followers.

"*Feacht*" and "*Sluaged*," or "expedition and hosting," covered not only the defence of the country, but offensive operations against an enemy, and were military services carried on by the tribesmen at their own charges. *Sluaged* also involved attendance at the king's council. It is termed in the later records "servitium Scoticanum," "forinsecum servitium," and "servitium in exercitu et auxiliis." The "Feacht" was the expedition within the kingdom or territory to repress rebellion or to enforce the law.

The "*Ich*" was apparently a tribute paid at intervals as an acknowledgment of subjection, and perhaps survived in the "*Calpe*" or "*Cawpe*" of more modern times.

In the reign of David I. we find a very great change introduced. The tenures belonging to the feudal system, such as military service, ward, and relief, were gradually supplanting the older tribal system. A national coinage for the first time enabled a small but ever-increasing proportion of the revenue to be paid in currency. The establishment of the burghs encouraged trade and commerce, and the "*Leges Burgorum*," of which a considerable part belongs to David's reign, contain probably the earliest provisions for a regular revenue which we have recorded. Though no burgh charter is extant belonging to such an early period, the references constantly made in the later grants of William the Lion to the privileges possessed by the burghs in the time of his grandfather show that if particular grants were not in existence some general body of legislation very favourable to municipal enterprise must have been in operation. No one can read the eulogium on David by Ailred of Rievaul, himself the friend and contemporary of the Scottish King, as it is recorded by Fordun, and confirmed by all that we know, without feeling that a new era in Scottish history commences with his reign. Society becomes more civilized, more settled, and therefore more progressive. "Ancient Gaelic Alban gradually fades into the background," and of that historical Scotland of which Edinburgh is the capital, and the "ruddy lion ramped in gold" the emblem, unquestionably David was the creator.

Among the various offices which can be traced back to his reign is that of the Chamberlain, whose primary duty was the collection, custody, and disbursement of the revenue, combined at first with a general supervision over the burghs from which a very considerable portion of that revenue was derived. The institution of this office is one of the distinctive features of the second period indicated above. The national revenue, from many sources and through various channels, came all eventually to the Treasury, and from the records, many of which are still extant, we have a tolerably clear idea of the fiscal system.

The immediate receivers of the funds were the Sheriffs, who by the time of Alexander III. had succeeded the Earls as collectors of the revenue; the *Ballivi ad extra*, or administrators of some of the Crown lands, or lands temporarily in possession of the Crown; the Justiciars, the Magistrates, and the Custumars or receivers of taxes of the burghs.

The sources of income were either ordinary or extraordinary.

The ordinary sources of income were (1) the rents of the lands in the possession of the Crown; (2) the payments due from the Thanages; (3) the casualties of ward, marriage, relief and non-entry exigible from time to time from the Crown vassals; (4) fines imposed on misdoers; (5) the escheats, or forfeited estates of attainted persons; (6) the rents derived from the royal burghs; (7) compositions payable for letters of gift, remissions, and legitimations; (8) the Castle wards, or dues exacted from lands in the immediate vicinity of some of the principal fortresses towards the expense of upholding them; (9) the duties payable on merchandise, called the great customs; (10) the profits arising from the coinage of money.

The extraordinary sources of income were special contributions for particular purposes, and were at first confined to the occasions recognized by the feudal law, such as the redemption of the king from captivity, the marriage of his daughters, etc.

Most of these sources of income were common to both the periods succeeding the reign of David I. Taxes in the modern sense of the word were not known till a later period.

It will be convenient to indicate shortly the general nature of each of these ordinary sources of revenue :—

(1) The Crown lands varied considerably at different periods, but in the time of the Alexanders were very extensive. They were partly in the actual occupation of the King (*terra dominica* or demesne), and cultivated by his tenants and *nativi*, and partly held as *thanages* by vassals who paid a rent instead of military service. A large portion of this revenue was at first paid in kind, such as oats, wheat, barley, malt, fodder, cattle, swine, and poultry. In some districts, such as Forfarshire, part of it was paid in cheese. When the Exchequer Rolls commenced considerable sums were paid in money, but the revenue from this source was very much curtailed by the dilapidation of the Crown lands before 1350.

(2) The thanages were lands which were granted feudally by charter, not for military services, but for the payment of an annual sum as *"census"* or feu-duty. The thanes held them *"in capite"* of the Crown, and paid their *"reddendo"* to the Sheriffs, who accounted for them to the Exchequer. These were gradually becoming extinct, and by the close of the reign of Alexander III. had almost all been converted into ordinary feudal tenures.

(3) The casualties of the feudal law payable by the vassal to the superior were a very considerable source of income. They were often gifted by the sovereign to individuals as rewards for particular services.

(4) Three times in each year the Justiciar, the supreme judge in criminal and civil cases, held Circuit Courts at the head burgh of each shire for the administration of law and the redress of grievances. At the time of the Alexanders there were three of these officers—the Justiciar of Scotland, of Lothian, and of Galloway. A large proportion of offences were punished by fines, and even murder, under the old law of "Cro" or "Wergild," could be compounded by the payment of a certain number of cattle, proportioned to the rank of the victim. The King's displeasure was often atoned for by a substantial fine. Thus in 1261 the Earl of Sutherland was fined £20, and in 1262 the Earl of Caithness paid 50 marks.

(5) Requires no particular explanation.

(6) The rents derivable from the royal burghs were, in the first place, an annual payment of five silver pennies from the holder of each rood of land in a burgh; secondly, the fines awarded in the Courts of the royal burghs; and thirdly, the burghal toll or *parva custuma*. About the beginning of the fourteenth century the burghs began to rent these petty customs from the Chamberlain, paying a fixed sum per annum and collecting them themselves; and some of the burghs, such as Aberdeen, in 1319, and Edinburgh, in 1329, had charters of feu farm from the Crown converting their tacks into perpetual rights, on payment of a fixed annual *reddendo*. In 1327 the aggregate revenue derived from this source amounted to £1,133 3s. 4d.

Apart altogether from their bearing on the national revenue, the accounts of these burgh rents afford us a very valuable index to the varying states of prosperity of the different centres of population at different times.

(7) The compositions payable for letters of gift and other concessions amounted to a considerable sum in some years, but varied so much that it is impossible to give an average.

(8) The castle ward payments were very trifling, and are only important for the principle recognized in their exaction.

(9) The King's "great custom" on merchandise exported must have originated in very early times, for grants to monasteries of one ship duty free are found in the reign of David I. It was collected at the ports of export by "custumars," who were generally one or two of the leading burgesses appointed for the purpose and remunerated by fees. It was mainly derived from three classes of exports —wools, woolfells (or sheepskins), and hides—and was payable about the time of Robert the Bruce at the rate of half a mark (6s. 8d. Scots) the sack of twenty-four stones on wool, at a quarter mark (3s. 4d.) on the hundred of woolfells, and at a mark (13s. 4d.) on the last of hides of twenty dacres, counting at that time probably ten to the dacre. The revenue derived from this source in 1327 amounted to £1,851 14s. 4¾d. from the ten principal burghs in the kingdom.

An important change took place in 1357. The defeat of the Scots at Durham and the capture of David II. led to a treaty finally concluded at Berwick, by which England was to receive 100,000 marks from Scotland in ten yearly instalments, commencing on the 25th of June, 1358. Among other expedients to raise this, in those days, enormous sum, the great customs were first trebled, and afterwards, in 1368, quadrupled; and the revenue from this source amounted sometimes to over £10,000 in the period between 1370 and 1379. These increased rates continued long after the ransom had been settled, for we find them in the succeeding reigns down to a late period.

In the time of James I. they produced in 1428 £6,912, the highest sum recorded in his reign, with an annual average of about £5,000. Certain additional customs were imposed by James I. He taxed the skins of the martin, polecat, otter, fox, rabbit, and deer. The produce was very trifling, the largest export being in rabbit skins, and the highest revenue recorded being £3 16s. 8d. in 1431. A further duty was imposed in 1424 of one shilling in the pound on the exportation of horses, sheep, and cattle, and a small duty on herrings exported of one penny on every thousand fresh fish sold, four shillings on each last of 12 barrels barrelled by Scotsmen, six if by foreigners, and fourpence on every thousand red herrings. A duty of two shillings in the hundred exported was also laid on "mulones," possibly cod. The second Parliament of the same year imposed a new custom of two shillings in the pound on woollen cloth exported, and another of two shillings and sixpence in the pound on salmon if bought by foreigners for exportation. Goods imported from England were also subjected to a duty of two shillings and sixpence in the pound. The average amount during the reign of James I. raised from the custom on woollen cloth was £300 per annum, and from salmon about £115 per annum. In 1428 a duty appears in the accounts on white salt at the rate of fivepence for every twelve chalders, but the Act of Parliament imposing it cannot now be found.

In the reign of James III. the gross revenue from the wool, woolfells, and hides fell on an average to less than £2,600. The revenue derived from the salmon and fish duties during the same period was about £310. Though at first put on the pound of value it was soon collected on the barrel, 12 of which made a last of Hamburg measure, and each was to contain 14 gallons. The custom was raised in 1480 to 4s. per barrel. In 1481 the custom of Lochfyne herrings amounted to the comparatively large sum of £34, and in 1487 the custom paid on the herrings of the "Lowis" (or Clyde lochs) at Dumbarton was as much as £379.

The revenue from the average gross customs in the reign of James III. amounted to about £3,300 annually.

In 1455 the whole customs of Scotland were annexed inalienably to the Crown.

From a complaint made by the Comptroller in 1542 it would appear that the total income from this source then amounted to about £5,000.

The later history of the customs after the accession of James VI. to the English throne must be dealt with hereafter.

(10) The profits arising from the coinage do not appear in the Rolls till the reign of David II. The earlier accounts are, unfortunately, lost. But, in 1358, Adam Thore, Warden of the Mint, accounted for £108 5s. 2d. profit to the King arising from a charge of seven pennies per pound weight of silver. As in 1367 the pound weight of silver was coined into 352 pennies, this was nearly equal to two per cent. In 1451 the seigniorage had risen to rather more than three per cent. In 1441 the seigniorage on gold was 16s. from each pound, and in 1525 it had mounted up to 26s. from each ounce of gold and 20s. from each pound weight of silver minted.

In 1593 the Mint was farmed out at a weekly rent of one thousand merks, and at the accession of James VI. to the English throne the seigniorage was fixed at 25s. 5d. per ounce from the gold coinage and one-twelfth part of the silver bullion for the silver coinage, including the expense of mintage. In 1683 the Commissioners appointed to report on the Mint affairs pronounced in favour of a free coinage, which was carried into effect in 1686.

Having reviewed the ordinary sources of income, we come now to those particular contributions, which were called for at uncertain intervals and on special occasions. There is positive evidence in the Cartulary of Scone that a national aid was asked for in Scotland during the reign of Malcolm IV. Another is said to have been granted by a National Assembly in 1174. The first tax of which we have any actual record was imposed in 1190 to assist William the Lion in paying off the 10,000 marks of sterlings which he agreed to pay to Richard I. of England to obtain the discharge of the Treaty of Falaise. In 1211 a further aid of 16,000 marks—10,000 of which were paid by the barons and 6,000 by the burghs—was granted to the same King. These aids were probably imposed by some sort of national authority, and in certain cases were assisted by voluntary contributions. This appears from a deed granted by William the Lion to the monks of the Cistertian Order, who claimed exemption from all taxation, but paid their share as a voluntary gift. Evidence exists in a charter granted to Aberbrothock by Alexander II. that aid had been called for by him in the beginning of his reign, perhaps on occasion of the marriage of his sister in 1224. When Alexander III. betrothed his daughter to Eric of Norway in 1281 he gave her a dowry of fourteen thousand marks of sterlings, and this sum would in all probability be raised in the same way. It is certain that during the reigns of the Alexanders there was a valuation roll or "extent" made containing the actual annual value at that time of a very considerable portion of the country. All the contributions up to this period were granted under the then common rule of the feudal system that in certain events the superior could call on his vassals to grant him special aid. It was not till after the successful conclusion of the War of Independence that we find a regular fixed sum granted to the Crown. Upon the 15th July, 1326, the Earls, Barons, Burgesses, and Freetenants of Scotland, assembled in Parliament at Cambuskenneth, granted to Robert Bruce for his life the tenth penny of their rents, "tam infra burgos et regalitates quam extra," according to the valuation made in the reign of Alexander III., with the provision that in the cases when the lands had been wasted by war the owner might apply to the Sheriff for a revaluation. This aid was given because the Crown lands were so wasted they could not support the necessary expenses of the King.

David II. was taken prisoner at the Battle of Durham in 1346, and in 1357 a tax was appointed to be imposed on all the rents and goods in the kingdom, for the purpose of paying his ransom of 100,000 marks of sterlings. The lands were to be taxed on their real value, and various other means were taken to raise this large sum of money. The financial embarrassment in which the country was placed by this burden was greatly increased by the debts and expenses incurred by the King. We get a glimpse of the comparative wealth of the various classes in Scotland at this period from the proportions in which the loans were to be gathered. The barons were to pay one-half, the clergy three-tenths, and the burghs two-tenths. The Parliament of October, 1370, imposed a special rate of one shilling in the pound; but, nevertheless, at David's death, on 22nd February, 1370-71, there still remained unpaid a balance of 48,000 marks.

When James I. returned from his captivity in England in 1424 his ransom, decently veiled under the name of "costage," was fixed at 60,000 marks of English standard money, to be paid in six yearly payments of 10,000 marks, but the last annual instalment was to be repaid as the dowry of the Queen. Of this large sum the burghs undertook to pay two-fifths, the other two Estates raising the remaining three-fifths. This affords us some idea of the comparative wealth of the different classes of population in Scotland at this period, and shows the progress made by the commercial interest since the middle of the fourteenth century, when their proportion of special taxes was only one-fifth, the barons paying one-half and the clergy three-tenths.

To raise this large sum special taxation was again imposed by Parliament, besides great additions to the customs. In every parish and burgh "extentors" were to be appointed, who, along with the priests, were to value each parish and town, and enter the rents of the lands, the names of the owners, their goods and substance in a book, to be presented to the King's auditors at Perth. On every pound's worth of rent and goods in burgh as well as out the tax was one shilling; every boll of wheat paid two shillings; of rye, sixteenpence; of oats, sixpence; every cow and her followers of two years and every ox, six shillings and eightpence; every sheep, one shilling; and so on. The expenses of the various embassies, such as that to the Duke of Burgundy in 1471, to France and Spain in 1488, to Denmark in 1491, and others seem to have been always defrayed by special taxation. In 1540 we find for the first time a sum imposed on the burghs for the purpose of furnishing "small artillery" (such as hagbuts and culverings), the other Estates providing them according to their valuation. Shortly afterwards a special sum of £16,000 was raised to assist in sending 1,000 horsemen to the Borders to repress incursions by "our aulde inymeis." These were to be engaged for three months, and each man was to receive four shillings a day. The proportion of the different Estates in these taxations for national defence are not indicated, but in 1580, when £40,000 was imposed for defence of the Borders, the Barons and

Freeholders paid two-sixths, the Church three-sixths, and the Burghs one-sixth.

Occasionally a general tax was raised for a more local purpose, such as the building of the bridge at Perth in 1578, the repair of the bridge of Don in 1587, and the protection of Dumbarton from the inroads of the Leven and the sea in 1607. But the most common cause for these special calls, more especially after the accession of James VI. to the English throne, was as aids not only for the contingencies recognized by the old feudal law, but to defray the Sovereign's expenses. Thus, in 1625, £400,000 was asked for to pay the debts of James VI. and the King's expenses at home and abroad. In 1630 the same amount was called for, nominally to defray the expenses of a proposed visit of the King to Scotland ; and special aids on various other pretexts occur in 1633, 1639, and 1640. No little dissatisfaction was caused by these exactions, and in 1643 an experiment was tried of asking for a loan of £800,000, one-sixth of which was to be advanced by the burghs and the remainder by the clergy, barons, and freeholders. The nature of the *loan* will be better understood when it is remembered that in the following year it was ordained that the names of those declining to *lend* were to be publicly read over in Parliament, their goods escheat, and their persons imprisoned.

During the Commonwealth matters were, if possible, worse. The Scotch members of Parliament sat in London, and their voice was little regarded. In 1652 they were ordered to raise £10,000 a month, and this sum is apparently sterling money, not Scots currency. The Scotch deputies prayed that Parliament would allow Scotland to be represented in the Parliament in London in proportion to its population, but this was refused by the English Committee, who decided that the number of members should be in proportion to the money raised from Scotland. On the 10th of March, 1652, the Scotch deputies protested against the heavy burden of taxation laid upon Scotland, but without any effect. In 1655 there is a return showing the division of this sum of £10,000 sterling among the various shires and burghs of the country. From this record we see that the shire of Ayr had to provide £545 12s. 2d. per month; the shire of Renfrew, £190 15s. 6d.; the shire of Lanark, £446 8s. 9d.; the shire of Edinburgh, £448 19s. 2d.; the city of Edinburgh, £540; the city of Perth, £60; and the city of Glasgow, £97 10s.

The money was raised on all personal as well as real estate, each £20 of personal estate having to bear the same charge as £1 of valued rent. Tenants, and all persons by whom annuities, pensions, stipends, or yearly rents or profits were payable, were to pay the tax and make deductions in reckoning with the owners and beneficiaries. The commissioners appointed to collect this tax in each shire or burgh had power to fine, imprison, sequestrate the estates, and poind and sell the effects of every person refusing to pay. There was also a power of quartering soldiers upon all persons in arrear. In 1656 an additional 6d. was assessed upon every £100 Scots of valued rent to defray the expense of arresting and punishing all vagrants and vagabonds.

At last General Monk became satisfied that Scotland could not really pay the sums demanded by the English Parliament, and he accordingly addressed a letter from Dalkeith in June, 1657, to Secretary Thurlow, in which he says :—

"I must desire you will consider this poore country, which truely I can make itt appeare that one way or other they pay one hundred pounds out of fower for their assessment : and the warre having soe much exhausted them as itt has done as by forfeitures and fines wee have much adoe to get itt uppe : and the soulders that receive itt had almost as well goe without their pay as gather itt uppe. And unlesse there bee some course taken that they may come in equality with England itt will goe hard with this people."

This shows that Scotland was more heavily taxed in proportion than England, and seems to have had some effect, for in the same year the proportion payable by Scotland was reduced to £6,000 per month. But in 1659 it was again raised to £12,000 a month, though probably never paid owing to the King's restoration in 1660.

Charles II. agreed to accept the sum of £40,000 a year from Scotland, but this sum was paid entirely by the Customs and Excise. A voluntary supply of £864,000 Scots was offered by the Scotch Parliament to the King in 1672 for the war against the States General, which was accepted. A supply was offered by the estates to James VII. in 1681 amounting to £1,800,000 Scots. In 1696 a supply of £1,440,000 Scots was granted to William II. for the security of the kingdom, but part of this was raised from the Excise. The last supply before the Union granted to Queen Anne was in 1706, and amounted to £577,066 13s. 4d. Scots.

The next great special source of revenue was the Excise, but this only came into operation at a comparatively late period. The first notice of it in the Records occurs in 1644, when Committees were appointed to consider whether money could be raised for the army by means of Excise. The result was that in the same year an Act of Parliament was passed imposing Excise duties on ale, aqua vitæ, wine, tobacco, etc. The rates were fourpence on every pint of ale or small beer; on foreign beer, a shilling; on French wine, 1s. 4d. per pint; on Spanish wine, 2s. 8d.; on aqua vitæ, 2s. 8d.; on every pound of tobacco, 6s.; on every ox, bull, or cow slaughtered above £16 in value, 20s.; if below £16 in value, 13s. 4d.; on every ell of silk stuff imported, from 6s. 8d. to 10s., according to value; on every beaver hat, 24s.; on every pair of silk stockings, 13s. 4d.; and similar duties on a long list of like objects. In Royal Burghs the Excise was to be collected by persons appointed by the Magistrates and Town Councils, who were allowed to retain 10 per cent. "for public, pious, and charitable uses within their burghs," and for payment of the sub-collectors' fees and expenses. The elders and deacons of every landward parish were to collect the Excise in their districts on similar terms. The original rates were from time to time varied and the articles added to or altered. In 1647 it was determined to farm the Excise, as being the most expeditious and easy way of raising the money. Sir William Dick paid, in 1648, 100,000 merks per annum for the Excise on wine for three years, and on the expiry of this term in 1651 it was granted to the Marquis of Argyll and Sir William Dick for five years at the yearly rent of 140,000 merks per annum, but adding the Excise in "strong waters."

We have a very good account of the fiscal state of Scotland at this period in the report made by Thomas Tucker in 1656. In May, 1655, Cromwell had appointed a Council of nine to administer the affairs of Scotland, who *inter alia* had full power and authority to collect the duties of Custom and Excise according to the rates in force in England.

In order to assist at the settlement of these matters the Lord-Protector and Council of England sent Mr. Thomas Tucker, then Register to the Commissioners of Excise in England, into Scotland, and appointed him a Commissioner during his residence in Scotland. From a letter from one of the Council to Secretary Thurlow it appears that before the Commonwealth the proceeds of the Excise on ale, beer, aqua vitae, and tobacco, the most important articles for excise purposes, had only amounted to about £1,100 sterling per month, and that the new Council hoped by greater strictness to double it. Their proceedings excited great discontent, as appears from the contemporary authors. Nicoll says—"The burdings of the land at this time (October, 1655) wes verie havie and grevous to be borne;" and Tucker in his report says the people were very impatient of the Excise duties to which they were not accustomed, and accounts for it through "an innate habit of theyr owne to bee crosse, obstinate, clamorous, and prone to apprehend every action an oppression or injury."

The first recommendation made by Tucker was that the Excise should be farmed out to the highest bidder, but that the term should be at first for four months, afterwards extended to one year. The result of this was that during the first four months

(19th September, 1655, to 19th January, 1655-56) the amount of Excise collected amounted to £10,471 9s. 10d., of which £9,824 was paid by the tacksmen and £647 9s. 10d. by collectors directly appointed by the Commissioners. The greatest difficulties in the collection were in the Western Highlands. For the counties of Argyll and Bute nobody would bid anything at all, and only nominal sums for Inverness, Ross, Sutherland, Cromarty, and Caithness. The Commissioners kept these in their own hands and sent out two collectors, "gentlemen of those countryes, one of which went clad after the mode of his countrye with belted playde, trowses, and brogues," as Tucker carefully informs us, but only succeeded in raising £27 in Argyll and Bute. In the second tacks for one year from January, 1655-6, to January, 1656-7, the whole sum raised by the Excise on ale, beer, and aqua vitae amounted to £35,054 8s. 8d. sterling.

Excise duties were also charged on salt, but the result was very small.

In 1661 the Excise on malt was charged at two merks per boll, and in 1693 an additional duty of 3d. per pint on ale and beer, and 2s. per pint on aqua vitæ and strong waters was imposed. These additional duties were continued by an Act of 1695. In January, 1701, the Excise was farmed for £30,000 sterling.

At the period of the Union the public revenue of Scotland from these various sources was estimated as follows, in sterling money :—

Excise, per annum	£50,000
Customs, per annum	50,000
Crown rents and casualties	8,500
Post office and casualties	2,000
Coinage and casualties	1,500
Land tax and casualties	48,000
Total	£160,000

CHAPTER VII.

TRADE AND COMMERCE.

WE are sometimes too apt to imagine that, because in our own times we have seen great progress made in the trading and commercial prosperity of this country, trade and commerce are things of modern growth. But a very superficial examination of by-gone days will serve to modify this opinion. If we give due consideration to the different state of population and the greater difficulties of transport, we hope to show that Scotland has been a commercial country from a very remote period.

And such an examination will bring out prominently another very important fact. There have been periods of great prosperity and periods of great depression in the past, just as there are at present, and just as there will be in the future. The union of the four independent kingdoms into the historical kingdom of Scotland was followed for a long time by a period of great prosperity. The disastrous events which followed the death of Alexander III. brought in their train a period of almost unexampled depression. And though our inquiry will not extend beyond the Union with England, the same results can be traced then. Whenever a few years of peace and tranquillity were enjoyed a time of commercial activity and national prosperity invariably followed. War and civil dissensions were just as certainly followed by a decline of trade and national adversity.

We shall not make any apology for entering somewhat minutely, especially in the earlier reigns, into this important subject. All the information we can now get is unfortunately too scanty, but, being derived from original records, it at least possesses the merit of being authentic. Perhaps the earliest historical notice of foreign trade in Scotland is found in Adamnan's " Life of S. Columba." He relates that in 597 when the holy man died his body was *" mundis involutum sindonibus."* As this fine linen was not at that time, so far as we know, a native manufacture, it was in all probability imported.

The long and peaceful reign of Macbeth affords indications of a considerable amount of wealth in the country, and of some intercourse with foreign nations. The

" Gret plenté
Abowndand, báth on land and se,"

which the old annalist chronicles, indicates the wealth

of the people; and Marianus Scotus, a respectable contemporary historian, relates that the Scottish King on his visit to Rome exercised a liberality in charity to the poor, remarkable even in that resort of wealthy pilgrims from every part of Christendom. "*Rex Scotie Machetad Rome argentum seminando pauperibus distribuit.*"

Malcolm III. encouraged Scottish merchants to import rich dresses and other foreign luxuries for the use of his Court, as is related in the life of his Queen, S. Margaret, given by the Bollandists in the "Acta Sanctorum."

One of the charters preserved in the treasury of Durham Cathedral shows that the Scottish King Edgar (1098-1107) granted the tolls or customs on the ships of certain parts of his kingdom to that church.

Alexander I. (1107-1124) possessed the foreign luxuries of an Arabian horse and Turkish armour, and he assigned to various parties the duties paid on trading vessels. In his reign Scotch pearls were exported to England. He also granted to the Monastery of Scone the custom of ships coming to the Tay; and addressed a writ to the merchants of England inviting them to trade and promising them his protection.

David I. (1124-1153) greatly encouraged trade and commerce, and it is recorded by his biographer,

Ailred of Rievaux, himself an eye-witness of what he states, that during the reign of that king Scotland was "no longer a beggar from other countries, but of her abundance relieving the wants of her neighbours—adorned with castles and cities, her ports filled with foreign merchandise and the riches of distant nations." There is trustworthy evidence of a considerable foreign trade in herrings in this reign. In the "Life of S. Kentigern," written in the twelfth century, it is incidentally noticed that at that time English ships (then, of course, foreign) and Flemish were accustomed to fish off the Isle of May.

The monks seem to have been active pioneers of commerce, as they were the first agriculturists and the earliest coal workers. David I. granted immunity from custom for one trading vessel to the monks of Dunfermline. The Abbot of Holyrood had several ships engaged in the fishing industry in the Firth of Forth. The canons of the same favoured foundation had an annual grant of one hundred shillings, then a very considerable sum, leviable on the first ships which came to Perth for the sake of trade—to procure them gowns. The Abbey of Cambuskenneth had a similar grant from Stirling, and the Bishop of Aberdeen had the tenth of the duty levied on ships coming to that port.

Berwick, then under Scottish rule, was in the twelfth century the great emporium of trade and commerce. The Norse writers tell us it had at that period many ships and more foreign commerce than any other port in Scotland. Torfæus relates that a great merchant of Berwick, called Cnut the Opulent, from his great wealth, had a ship which was captured at sea by Erlend, the Norse jarl of the Orkneys. On board the vessel was the merchant's wife, returning probably from a pilgrimage. On hearing of the disaster Cnut immediately fitted out a fleet of fourteen ships, fully equipped and armed, and at once set out in pursuit of the pirates. The end of the story is unfortunately not given. William the Lion (1165-1214) reigned for nearly forty-nine years, and Scotland made great progress during his long and wise rule. The various grants paid to Richard of England show the increase of wealth in the country, and the proportion of the revenue paid by the burghs, already alluded to, is a proof that the trading community was prospering more than any other class. About 1182 the monks of Melrose had a charter from Philip, Count of Flanders, enjoining all his men not to dare to exact from them any toll or duty on land or sea, but to give them every facility for trading in the Low Countries.

The regulations recorded in the "Assise Willelmi Regis" refer frequently to merchants and traders.

The merchants of the realm were required to have their guild, and to have full liberty to buy and sell in all places within the liberties of the burghs. Another law practically conferred a monopoly of trade on these merchant guilds. Further regulations in the interest of the burghs provided that stranger merchants from foreign nations were not to trade except within the burghs, and *chiefly* to the merchants. They were not permitted to sell cloth " in penny worthis " but wholesale.

The records relating to Scotland preserved in the Public Record Office, London, recently calendared by Mr. Joseph Bain, and published by authority of the Lords Commissioners of the Treasury, under the direction of the Deputy-Clerk Register of Scotland, throw a considerable light on the trade and commerce of the country at this period. Thus, we find that in 1205 a writ is noted from the King of England commanding W. de Wrotham and G de Luscy forthwith to deliver up and restore two Scottish ships, taken at Sandwich, laden with merchandise, which the merchants could show was their own. In 1212 we again find three burgesses of Dundee sued by a London merchant for a debt of forty pounds. A further proof of the commerce of this reign is found in a letter written by William the Lion to the Norse Harold, jarl of Orkney and Caithness, entreating his favour for the monks of

Scone, who traded largely by sea to their possessions in the north.

Alexander II. (1214-1249) reigned for thirty-four years, during which the prosperity of the country was still increasing. This is proved in the first place by the large amounts of money which the king was enabled to spend. He gave his second sister 10,000 marks, besides lands, on her marriage; and also gave to Henry III. of England 500 marks for the wardship of his youngest sister's husband, then under age. A further evidence of Scottish trading enterprise is afforded us by the publication of the records already alluded to. We find there that in 1214 the bailiffs of the port of Southampton were commanded to deliver up all merchant vessels, including those of the King of Scotland, and let them freely depart. Similar orders were given to the bailiffs of Lynn and the Sheriff of Norfolk. In the same year the King of England ordered the Justiciar of Ireland to allow the men of Alan of Galloway, to come to Ireland and return with the ship which the said Alan had taken at Kirkcudbright, and to allow him to have his merchandise in the said ship.

From the same source we get evidence of a very considerable trade with Ireland at this time. Special permissions seem to have been required for those desiring to buy corn, meal, or other articles of food in that country, and these are frequently recorded.

"The first religious body," says Mr. Bain in his interesting preface, "to obtain such permission was that of Vauday (Vallis Dei), situated at Kar, in Galloway, on 15th February, 1220-21, to last for four years from Easter." Another Galloway churchman, the Abbot of Dundrennan, had a similar grant for three years shortly after. The bailiffs of King's Lynn, a port of large trade with Scotland, were commanded on 8th August, 1223, to allow the wines, etc., for the King of Scots private use to be shipped, and all the small Scotch vessels to depart. They were also commanded to release corn-laden vessels for Scotland and Norway. In August, 1224, the abbots of Melrose and Cupar had leave to trade beyond seas; a Dieppe merchant to bring wine for Scotland to Berwick; and the bailiffs of Yarmouth were commanded to release Scottish merchant vessels and fishing vessels of all countries. The bailiffs of Southampton were ordered to release John Ruffus, a Scottish merchant of Berwick, and his ship, the *Portejoye*. In April, 1225, the abbots of Melrose and Cupar had leave to send wool to Flanders; and in May of the same year Alexander of Dunwich, a Scottish merchant, was allowed to carry a cargo of barley and beans northward from Lynn.

In 1226 the Abbot of Holmcultram had leave to buy corn in Ireland till Henry of England attained his majority; and his neighbour of Glenluce, in Galloway, had the same permission for a year, repeated in 1227. John of Dunwich and Hugh, son of Odo, two Scottish shippers of corn, were respectively allowed to depart from Sandwich and Lynn. Joce of Dunwich had leave to sail with a cargo of Gascon wine for Scotland, and a corn vessel bound for Scotland was released from Lynn in the same year.

In September, 1227, the monks of Kilwinning had leave to buy corn in Ireland for a year, a privilege repeated in 1252. In 1229 a Berwick merchant's wool, arrested at Dover, was ordered to be released on his proving his nationality; and three Scottish ships with cargoes of corn, wine, and salt were similarly released at Lynn. In the same year Simon of St. Andrews, a merchant of the King of Scots, had leave to trade in England for a year with his vessel; and the Constable of Dover was ordered to deliver to a Berwick merchant his hides and wool which had been arrested at Romney.

The Abbot of Melrose's vessel, of which Friar William de Bowden was the supercargo, was allowed in 1230 to trade in England for a year; and by the direct intervention of the King of Scots a strict inquiry was ordered to be made as to the plundering of the ship of John Ruffus, his burgess of Berwick, when she was in danger near Yarmouth, and restitution was to be made. The vessels of six traders of Lynn were permitted to sail for Scotland and Norway.

In September, 1237, after the treaty at York, the English King commanded the Mayor of Dublin to release the goods of Scottish merchants arrested on account of William de Marisco's piracies, and the Mayor of Drogheda to release the ship and goods of the merchants of Ayr so seized. Erkin, of Kirkcudbright, and Richard Ruffus got leave to go with their vessels to Ireland to trade for corn.

In 1242, we find a reference made to a ship freighted from Scotland to the port of London, and in the same year there is a curious record proving the existence of a Scotch colony of traders at Dunwich, who seem to have done a considerable business. The Mayor was a Scotchman, "Lucas le Scot," and another, "Gerard Scot," is also named.

In August, 1246, we have evidence of some trade between France and Scotland, for on the first of that month the King of Scots guaranteed some debts due by merchants of Perth to traders in Bordeaux, and in 1249 the Justiciar of Lothian became similarly bound for debts owing in Scotland to Peter de Camera, a merchant of Bordeaux. A considerable light is thrown on the commercial condition of Scotland six centuries ago by the Statuta Gilde, or "Laws of the Merchants of Berwick," which were enacted in 1249, during the mayoralty of Robert de Bernhame. Their importance is increased by the fact that they seem to have been recognized by all the trading towns of Scotland; and, although bearing to have been recorded at the date given above, they had in all probability been in existence from a considerably earlier period.

About the middle of the thirteenth century Berwick was undoubtedly the principal port in Scotland. It is described in the chronicle of Lanercost as a "city so populous and of such trade that it might justly be called another Alexandria, whose riches were the sea, and the waters its walls. In those days its citizens being most wealthy and devout, gave noble alms." For these reasons, and also because the "Lawis of the Gild" were the earliest effort of local self-government among the commercial communities of Scotland, the code is well worth a somewhat minute examination.

These laws are recorded in Latin, but an ancient translation into the vernacular Scottish has also been preserved. They bear to have been ordained and constituted by Robert de Bernhame, Mayor of Berwick, Simon Maunsel, and "othir gude men of the said burgh," with the object "that throu mony body is in a place gaderit togidder thru the relacion of ane til an other may folow vnite and concord, ane will, and ferme and sekyr lufe ilk ane till other." In order to secure these laudable objects stringent provisions were adopted against transgressors. If a guild brother offended another by contemptuous talk (*verbotenus diliquerit*) he was to be fined forty silver pennies for each on each of the three first occasions, and if the offence was continued he was to be specially judged by the Alderman,[47] Farthingmen (the wardmen or those who had charge of different quarters of the town, or, according to others, the treasurers), the Dean of Guild, and " the laf of the brether," and amerced accordingly. If a member struck another, he was to be fined half a mark besides paying amends to the injured brother. If blood was drawn the offender was to pay two hundred and forty silver pennies as a penalty, besides satisfaction to the assaulted brother at the will of the Alderman and brethren. No merchant, when bargaining, was allowed to carry a knife with a point, on a penalty of twelve sterlings. Provision was also made for decent conduct and against public nuisance, and offenders were to be fined four silver pennies for each offence. *Si quis minxerit super calciamenta sua in vili modo aut super pariates domus Gilde nostre . . . . emendet in quatuor denariis.* An entrance fee of 480 sterlings had to be paid by each member unless he was the immediate descendant of one already a member; but if any brother became sick or fell into poor circumstances through no fault of his own he had a claim to be relieved by the guild at the will of the Alderman and brethren. A singular regulation provided that in the case of a brother in poor circumstances leaving a daughter unprovided for the guild supplied her with a husband, or enabled her to enter a religious house at her pleasure. Poor brethren were to be buried with decency according to the rites of the Church; and if any brother, being in the town, neglected to come to the funeral, he was fined in a boll of barley malt. Provision was made for helping any members who were "vexit or chalangit" outside the town; but if any one ceased to become a member, or was expelled, no one was to assist him in any difficulty or peril— "he sall haue na help of thaim." When any matter occurred requiring the advice of the brotherhood, a little bell was first rung through the town, and then the great bell in the bell-house was tolled thrice, with a reasonable interval, and any one failing then to attend was fined twelve pennies. If any one spoke in the Assembly, or in the Courts, except the pursuer and defender, or their advocates and the bailies, or unless he was specially called on, he was to be fined ninety-six silver pennies.

To ensure public health, all lepers and infected persons were to be thrust out by the serjeants of the town beyond the walls, but a hospital was provided outwith the town by voluntary contributions for such unfortunates. Any one "daring or presuming" to deposit filth or any dust or ashes on the street or the market place, or on the banks of the river, were to be fined ninety-six silver pennies.

To ensure the dignity of the brethren, every one who had goods in his possession to the extent of ten pounds or upwards was to provide for himself "a seemly horse," on pain of a heavy fine.

The trading regulations are worth notice. No one was allowed to buy or sell hides, wool, or wool skins to sell again, except a member of the guild or a " stranger merchant." No shoemaker was allowed to tan any hides, except those that had horns and ears of equal length. No tanner was permitted to salt hides. No butcher was allowed to buy wool or hides unless he " abjured his axe and swore never to lay hands on beast." No skinner, nor glover, nor any one, was to make wool of any skins from Whitsunday till Michaelmas, but to sell the skins " as he best might." If any one took money from a stranger merchant on commission, and of it took a profit above the market, he was to be fined for the first and second offence, and for the third expelled the guild for ever, unless pardoned. No one was allowed to purchase herrings or other fish, or any other merchandise, such as corn, beans, pease, or salt, coming by sea until the ship was berthed and the oars taken out. Any one offending was to be fined a cask of wine, or expelled the town for a year and a day. Any one who had legitimately bought such goods was obliged to sell at the price he had bought to any guild brother who desired it for his own sustenance or that of his household up to three-fourths of the investment, but any one who got any goods for this reason and sold them again was fined a cask of wine.

Payment for merchandise was made on delivery, and when a bargain was completed by giving "God's penny or any siluer in arles" he who refused to implement it was fined in a cask of wine to the guild. But if the article contracted for was "good above and worse below" arbiters were appointed to judge in the matter. Every morning at a certain hour—not recorded—the great bell rung in the bell-house, and no one was allowed to buy anything brought to the town for sale before that time. No married woman was to buy wool in the street, and no merchant was to have more than one servant to buy wool or hides. If any one went and procured a stranger to plead against his neighbour, or plotted against the guild, he was to be fined a cask of wine.

The government of the community was confided to twenty-four "good men of the better, more discreet, and more trustworthy of the burgh chosen thereto," along with a mayor and four bailies, who were elected "at the sight and by the consideration of the whole community."

Any one who revealed the secrets of the guild was reputed infamous (*infamis reputatur*).

Some later regulations of the same guild may be conveniently noticed here. Merchants who sold wine were to pay one penny for each cask taken from or put on board a ship, or exposed for sale in their booths, to the town, and another penny and a halfpenny for drink-money. Butchers were not to buy beasts on their way to market, nor in the market until after dinner. No merchandise coming by sea was to be bought except at the ship's side, and only between the rising and setting of the sun.

In the Chartulary of Glasgow there are some ordinances which are believed to date from the thirteenth century, if not earlier. They provide that no bailie should keep a tavern or sell bread "on pain of the king's amercement unforgiven," and no one outwith a burgh was to have a brew-house, except those who had the right to pit and gallows (that is, except barons), and then only one was allowed for private use.

Some curious facts regarding early Scottish commerce can be gathered from the "Assisa de Tolloneis," which shows the various articles of export and import in use. Though the existing MSS. are not prior to the reign of Robert the Bruce, they may safely be used for the earlier period of which we are now treating. From that record we find that skins of foxes, beavers, cats, hares, and such like small wild animals were articles of ordinary trade, as well as hides, deer skins, and sheep skins. Corn, salt, malt, beans, pease, leeks, onions, garlic, butter, cheese, iron, pottery, and mercery were commonly exposed for sale in the burgh markets. Horses, cattle, sheep, and swine brought into a burgh for sale paid duty. Herrings, salmon, ling, coal fish (*colemoth*), cod (*kelyng*), haddock, whiting, and oysters were ordinary articles of diet, and bought and sold freely.

Brazil (a wood used for dyeing red), madder (a plant used for the same purpose), wood, wax, pepper, cumin seed, alum, ginger, setwell (*curcuma zedoaria*, a plant which is a powerful sudorific), rice, figs, and raisins, all mentioned as occurring in the markets, represent a considerable amount of foreign natural products. Canvas, nets (*kellis*), thread for nets, linen thread, battens, rafters or spars (*cheueronys*), and knives were probably foreign manufactured goods, though possibly of native origin. Ornamental leather (*cordwan*, so called from Cordova in Spain), kitchen utensils (*battry*), caldrons, brass pots, locks, and oil were almost certainly foreign.

In the "Custuma Portuum," which is traditionally ascribed to David I., certain duties are imposed on shipping, which incidentally prove the existence of considerable commerce. Thus, in the port of Berwick, a merchant ship of England, "or ony oute kynryke," paid twelve silver pennies for its berth, while the Scottish ship only paid four. If the vessel was laden with wine, or honey, or oil, or any other merchandise stored in tons, and if any of it was sold, the "tome [48] ton" became the king's property, for what purpose it is difficult to imagine. The last matter to be noted in this reign throws a curious light on Scottish enterprise in a different direction. In 1249 the Earl of St. Pol and Blois was preparing to accompany the King of France to the Holy Land, and as the Crusaders then took with them their horses they required vessels of a considerable size. The ship of the French Earl was built at Inverness, probably on account of its proximity to the great forests of the North; artificers were sent from Flanders, Marseilles, and Genoa to assist the native workmen, and the result was, in the language of Matthew Paris, our authority for the event, "navis miranda."

The reign of Alexander commenced on the 8th of July, 1249, and closed on the 19th of March, 1285-6, and during that period Scotland continued to make a constant improvement in civilization and prosperity. The scanty materials at our disposal indicate an equal progress in trade and commerce.

In 1250 the Abbot of Glenluce again had leave for seven years to get corn in Ireland for the use of the monastery; and in the following March Robert le Stater, a Scotch merchant of Berwick, had a grant of his ship and cargo, cast ashore near Marbletorp, in Lincolnshire, by stress of weather. The ship was plundered by the coast men, and the proceedings in the King's Court at Westminster are interesting as showing the value of a ship and cargo of a Scottish merchant in the thirteenth century. The mast and sail yard were valued at 40s.; the hull and small furniture at £6; a sail, 4 marks; two anchors, ropes, and wreckage, £4; the chests, cloth, etc., composing the cargo, were taken away, so that no value could be put on them. These values were assessed by special parties named, on the oaths of the mariners and others of Grimsby and Boston. The sums named were all to be paid to the owner by the district where the plunder had taken place.

In 1258 we get another glimpse of the Scotch community at Dunwich in some singular proceedings before the Sheriff of Suffolk. A special jury was summoned to inquire into the cause why the goods and merchandise of Reginald of Acre, valued at one hundred marks and more, had been arrested by Lucas the Scot. From the proceedings recorded it appeared that Reginald and his wares duly arrived at Dunwich. And Lucas the Scot hearing it said that Reginald was a famous chirurgeon, spoke to him as to curing his wife, who was ill. Reginald took up his residence in Lucas's house, and committed all his wares to the care of Lucas, and Richard his son. He prescribed for the sick woman for four days, but she, finding herself no better, expelled him from the house. He then applied for his goods, but they declined to give them up. At the sitting of the Court, Lucas and Richard professed to produce the goods, but Reginald, on seeing them, swore they were not all there, especially naming ten gold rings with precious stones, certain ornamental buttons of crystal, and other articles. The jury found that there was a shortcoming in the goods, and remitted the case to the King's Court. Lucas seems to have got into frequent legal troubles. He paid a fine of three marks of gold in October, 1258; and in 1260 was accused of a transgression against Tidemann and Salomon, of Hamburg. The Mayor and community of Hamburg took up the quarrel, and arrested, according to "merchants' law," the goods of English merchants trading to that port. But these were released on the receipt of a letter from the King of England stating that the aggrieved merchants had been fully satisfied of their chattels and losses by Lucas. In the following year another example occurs of the exercise of "merchants' law." The English King addressed a writ to the Mayor of

Lynn, setting forth that Henry le Tenturer, Richard Robert le Mercer, John Lummelucas, John of Beverley, and Alan of Bedford, all merchants of Scotland, had abstracted from Ralf of Stannford 14 marks 4 shillings, and, as the King of Scotland had failed to do justice, he commanded the Mayor and Bailiffs to arrest all Scotch goods at the fair till Ralf obtained justice.

Towards the close of 1258, on March 18, Walter Cumin, Earl of Menteith, Alexander Cumin, Earl of Buchan, and their friends and allies made a bond of mutual alliance and friendship with Lewellyn, Prince of Wales, David ap Grufud, his brother and others. Among other matters it was provided that Welsh merchants should have safe conduct to come and trade in Scotland, and that Scotch merchants should have full liberty and encouragement to go and trade in Wales.

The abbot and monks of Arbroath in 1260 had a confirmation of a charter granted to them by the English King John at the instance of William the Lion, by which they were given permission to buy and sell for their own use throughout all England, free of toll, duty, or custom, saving only the liberty of the city of London. The merchants of Berwick were at the same time freed from all arrestment in England for any debt for which they were not guarantees or principal debtors, unless it was reasonably established that they had failed in justice to their creditors. The bailiffs of all the ports of England, Ireland, and Gascony were commanded in 1263 to seize a certain vessel belonging to John the Scot, merchant of Berwick, which had been illegally taken possession of by the crew, who were wandering about "as vagabonds and fugitives on the sea," and restore the ship and her cargo to the owner.

A curious fact about Haco's invasion of Scotland in 1263 is given in a letter from Henry III. of England to Magnus, King of Norway, in 1266. The Norwegian King had sent an Envoy to England to remind Henry of a proposal made during the lifetime of Haco that Norwegian merchants sustaining losses in England should be re-imbursed if the same was done to English merchants in Norway, and complaining that nothing had been done. The English King gave as his reason for not doing anything that some English vessels had been arrested in Norway to be used in the war against Scotland and against Alexander, King of Scots, his son-in-law, which was hurtful to both. In the treaty between Scotland and Norway, concluded the same year, provision was made for the security and protection of the persons, vessels, and goods of the merchants of either country who might be wrecked.

In 1285 an extraordinary letter was addressed to Alexander III. by a Spanish merchant and ship-owner, which is still preserved in the Public Record Office, London. It is written in Spanish, and narrates how the ship sailed from Bordeaux for London and was driven by a tempest far out of her course to the isles of "Hincha Guala," where they found a good harbour, and remained there till the storm was over. Then there came the men of "Alan Radric" with a sealed letter offering to show them a better port and to take care of their goods. They accordingly went, and Alan took out all their wares and left only two men in the vessel, and she went ashore and became a total wreck; whereupon Alan took for himself all the goods, including 8 tuns of wine, 300 dozen of Cordova skins, a great quantity of raisins and dates, a bale of silk, shields and armour for 30 men, and 20 silk banners. Besides this, the crew lost two changes of clothes for each man, and a considerable sum of money which they had to spend. The Spanish captain concludes his letter with the following prayer:—" And Lord for the great mercy in you make Alan and his men come before you and tell these things in our presence; and Lord do me justice in your Court."

The death of Alexander III. closed the most prosperous period in the history of Scotland till comparatively recent times. More especially the commercial progress which has been noticed received a severe check by the political troubles which followed.

In 1288 Edward I., in his ordinance for regulating the trade of Ireland, prohibited the merchants of that country from carrying corn, victuals, or other merchandise to "his enemies of Scotland." As peace still continued between the two countries, these "enemies" must have been the adherents of Robert Bruce, who had entered into a confederacy in 1286 to disappoint Edward's views as to the disposal of the young Queen.

A few years later, in 1293, Albert the Scot and John the Scot, merchants of Piacenza, had license to trade in England during the King's pleasure. Immediately afterwards we find, in a commercial treaty between England and Flanders, in 1297, Edward I. stipulating that the Flemings should have free and secure trade in Scotland. Either this stipulation had been rescinded or had not been given effect to, for in 1305 Robert, Count of Flanders, asked that his men might be allowed to trade with the Scots. This request was probably not granted, at least judging by the policy Edward displayed now towards Scotland, and by what afterwards occurred. There are extant letters of safe conduct in favour of Jacques Dribrod, burgess of St. Omer, and his sons, to trade for two or three years in Scotland. The writ to the Scottish Chancellor bears that the King has granted these with much regret, and only at the special request of his faithful and loyal John de Menteith. Almost directly afterwards he commanded the Chancellor of Scotland to seize the goods, effects, or debts of the great trading communities of the Pullici and Rembertini,[49] on the pretext that they were due monies to various parties and had not satisfied them. In all probability they had been giving assistance to the Scots against the English.

In 1313, Edward II. wrote, on the 15th February, to the Count of Flanders, complaining that his subjects still traded with the Scots, and supplied them with provisions, armour, and other necessaries. He wrote again on the 1st of May pointing out that thirteen Flemish ships had sailed from the Swyn for Scotland with arms and provisions. No answer is recorded to these complaints, and probably none was given, for on June 19 the English King ordered the arrest of all Flemish vessels in English ports.

Following out his vindictive policy, the English King again wrote on the 25th March, 1319, to Robert, Count of Flanders, and the towns and communities of the Low Countries, to cease trading with the people of Scotland; and the answers of several of these have been preserved. John, Duke of Brabant, assures Edward that the Scots will have no aid from his territories, and the burgesses of Yprès and Mechlin write to the same effect. But the Count of Flanders declares that his country is open to all comers, and he will not deny entrance to "the subjects of the King of Scots"; and the inhabitants of Bruges make an intimation to the same effect.

Almost the only other recorded trace of Scottish commerce during the reign of Robert Bruce is found in an agreement made between him and the King of Norway in 1312, providing *inter alia* for redressing some injuries suffered by merchants of St. Andrews in that country.

The reign of David II. marks a very important era in the early trade of Scotland. In 1347 a formal agreement was made between the merchants of Scotland and the burgesses of Middleburgh in Zealand for establishing a staple there. The agreement was confirmed in a Parliament held at Dundee on the 12th November, and the Scots were empowered to appoint a "mayor"—an officer probably of the same sort as the "conservator" of Scottish privilege afterwards so common in Holland—to look after their interests.

A further proof of increasing commercial activity is found in another Act of Parliament, passed in 1357, ordaining that all stranger merchants were to be received peaceably and encouraged to come to the country for the purposes of trade. It may be as well at this stage to explain the methods of international commerce in the fourteenth century and the peculiar terms which will constantly meet us in our inquiry. With regard to "staple," Gerard Malynes, merchant.

I

in his treatise on the *Lex Mercatoria*, published at London in 1622, thus defines the term:—" The most ancient foundation of merchants and merchandising in this kingdome, both for trade and government, had by continuance of time before King Henrie the Third, did obtaine the name of staple. The commodities of the realme, as wools, leather, woolfells, and other commodities, were called staple merchandise; the ports from whence the said commodities were to bee transported were called staple ports; the places of residence of these merchants, both within this land and beyond the seas, were called the staples; the laws and ordinances made by the said merchants were called staple laws; under their government, consisting of a maior, two constables, and other officers, hath the trade of this kingdome time out of mind flourished." The Mayor had authority to determine all disputes amongst the merchants of the staple; but if the dispute arose between a stapler and a stranger merchant two impartial stranger merchants were joined with him.

Unfortunately, the records of the agreement as to the Scottish staple between the merchants of Scotland and the town of Middleburgh have not been preserved, but some idea of it can be got from a later transaction of a similar sort described in the inventories of the charters of the burgh of Edinburgh in 1540. By this contract, which was made anent the staple with the city of Antwerp, it was provided that the "Nation of Scotland" should have "a fair and pleasant house" for the residence of their Mayor (then called Conservator), "in which house they might also lodge their packets and merchandise, and otherwise use it at their pleasure during their residence in the said town." The Magistrates of Antwerp agreed to "commune" with the owners of houses in any part of the town which the Scottish merchants might select, so that the Scots "should have reason to be contented with the price of the said houses," for their lodging. They were to be exempt from all excise of wine, ale, or beer consumed in said house, provided none other than Scots frequented such. When a fleet came from Scotland, and the merchants were too numerous for one house, the Burgomaster and Council agreed to assign two or three more as might be required for the occasion under the same regulations.

All complaints, questions, or causes between one Scotsman and another were to be decided summarily and finally by the Conservator, the Burgomaster and Council binding themselves to carry the sentence into effect. But when a stranger commenced a suit against any of the Scots nation he was required to raise it in the Conservator's Court in the first instance; but after the judgment was given either party, thinking himself aggrieved and wishing to have further trial, might then go to the Burgomasters by way of appeal. If any Scot commenced an action against a burgess of Antwerp or any stranger, it was to be tried by the Burgomaster and not by the Conservator.

Wharves were set apart for the special use of the Scottish merchants, who were permitted to sell and dispose of all kinds of merchandise. If salt fish were sold by retail, it was provided they should be first passed by the Cure Masters of Fish. The wages of labourers and working men were to be fixed by the Magistrates of Antwerp "to the reasonable satisfaction and content of the Scots nation."

The Scottish fleet of trading ships was to be piloted free of cost from the place of La Vere or Flushing according as the ships should arrive. If any Scottish ship was stranded between La Vere or Flushing and Antwerp the city was to furnish all assistance and contribute to the expenses caused by the occurrence and delay. Strict regulations were laid down as to the Scottish merchants being in no ways molested or unduly hindered by the Customs officials, and if any goods were plundered between Antwerp and La Vere or Flushing the city became bound to make good the loss.

This agreement with Antwerp was followed in the next year by another with Middleburgh, which probably was more favourable to the Scottish merchants than the one of 1347. It provided that the Council of Middleburgh, " for the love they did bear to the kingdom of Scotland, being desirous to continue the ancient amity and goodwill that always subsisted between them," should give to the said Scottish merchants "all possible aid, assistance, and advice at all times whenever they should be required thereto." Moreover, they promised to provide, " without any charge to the kingdom of Scotland, a very gentle house worthy of the said nation." In addition, they agreed to erect and furnish a chapel, to the honour of God, with an altar and all necessary ornaments for the convenience of the said Scottish nation. The other provisions were similar to those already noticed.

Middleburgh, though it must always be a most interesting place to Scottish merchants, is now greatly fallen from its position as a commercial centre. In the fourteenth century it was one of the chief trading ports of the Netherlands. Lodovico Guicciardini (quoted by Cosme Innes) speaks highly of its admirable situation and of its great ship canals, by which great vessels could pass from the port to the town. At the other end of the canal, about a league distant, was Campvere, a place of which we shall hear a great deal during the following century.

The establishment of the Scottish staple at Middleburgh in 1347 was followed by more cordial relations between Scotland and England. In 1362 Edward III. ordered that the ships, merchandise, etc., of the Scottish traders should not be molested at English ports, and the records of the period show an increased number of safe-conducts granted to Scots for the purpose of trading in England. Thus in 1358 Andrew de Murref and Alan Erskin, and in 1362 John de Petscoty and twenty-seven others, all described as merchants of Scotland, were guaranteed safe ingress and egress to England for commerce.

But though these are signs of a gradual increase of Scottish trade and commerce, it was still a long way behind the rest of Europe for more than a century. The author quoted above, Guicciardini (a nephew of the historian), writing in the middle of the sixteenth century, gives a vivid description of the trading communities of the Low Countries, and a detailed account of the exports and imports of the principal countries in Europe, with an estimate of their value. He estimates the trade between England and the Netherlands at twelve millions of scudi yearly (about £3,000,000 sterling); but he classes the trade with Scotland, Ireland, and Barbary together as not worth the trouble of calculating, it was comparatively so small.

The fifteenth century is singularly deficient in any notices of Scottish trade and commerce. In 1487 the Parliament of James ratified and approved certain articles presented by the Convention of Burghs. The first was in reference to letters of marque granted by the King of the Romans. It was agreed to send an embassy with as much speed as possible to the said King, the expenses of which were to be divided among the burghs. It was next provided that no one was to trade to Flanders, Holland, or Zealand, except "famous and woureschipfull men haifand ilk ane of them awne half a last of gudis," who were to be free men of a burgh and indwellers within the same.

Some few scanty notices occur in the Acts of Parliament and other records showing that foreign trade existed, if it did not flourish. Thus in 1454, in 1478, in 1481, and in 1482 Acts of Parliament were passed to encourage the import of victuals. Spears of six ells in length only were to be imported by an ordinance of 1471. The Acts of 1464, 1466, and 1483 prove the existence of an export trade in wool, skins, hides, cloth, and salmon. Adulterated wines were prohibited by an enactment in 1482. The export of horses under three years of age, of cattle, and of tallow was prohibited by Acts in 1424 and 1468. In 1427 merchants were permitted to carry their merchandise for one year in foreign vessels if no Scottish ones could be had. In 1491 it was ordered that the Isle of "Inchgarde," in the Forth, should be fortified to protect merchant shipping, and certain dues payable by ships seeking its protection were fixed.

Some idea of the commerce of this obscure period may be gathered from the returns from the Customs as recorded in the Rolls of the Exchequer. The duty on wool was 2 marks on each sack (of 24 stones); 1 mark for the long hundred of woolfells, and 4 marks for the last of hides (each last containing about 200 hides). The revenue derived from these is estimated by Mr. Burnett to be, on the average, rather under £2,600 per annum, as against £7,640 in the reign of Robert II. Woollen cloth was charged with an *ad valorem* duty of 2s. in the pound, and the annual average of the export dues from all the ports in Scotland was only about £108. The next important article of commerce was salmon, the duty on which was 2s. 6d. in the pound, and the annual average income from which was about £310.

The returns of the import duties show a trade in wheat, malt, barley, beer, wines, salt, soap, cups (*ciphi*), and the total from the whole Customs amounts to about £3,300 yearly.

The sixteenth century develops a considerable increase in the foreign trade of Scotland; and we have now the guidance and assistance of the very valuable Records of the Convention of Royal Burghs.

The first year of the century it was ordered by the Provost of Edinburgh that nobody except a burgess dwelling in a burgh should trade with France or Flanders.

In 1529 John Campbell of Lundy was sent to Flanders to negotiate a treaty of commerce between the "nation of Scotland" and the Emperor; and the following were the principal points on which he was to insist :—

First, that one payment of custom should free the goods of the nation of Scotland from every other charge ; secondly, that the said custom should not be greater than it was of old; thirdly, that all the Scotch merchants should be well dressed for the honour of the realm; and, if not, the Conservator was empowered to seize and sell enough of their merchandise to fit them out reputably; and, lastly, that no Scottish merchant should raise any action against another in Flanders, except in the Conservator's Court.

At a Convention of the Royal Burghs held at Edinburgh in 1539, Master William Thompson, canon in Our Lady Kirk of Antwerp, appeared and expressed for the community of Antwerp their great desire to have the staple of the Scottish nation fixed there, and their readiness to do everything they could to meet the wishes of the Scottish merchants. The matter was delayed to give the burghs an opportunity of considering the proposals from Antwerp. Two years later the Convention agreed to have the staple in Flanders, at whichever town would grant the greatest privileges. The trade with France was evidently now of some importance, for in the same Convention the burghs agreed to defray the expenses of a "great personage" to go to the King of France for the purpose of getting a new imposition lately placed on trade with France modified; and if "a personage of less degree" was to be sent, the Convention agreed to pay whatever portion of his expenses the town of Edinburgh might agree to. Some years later (in 1563), it was agreed by the burghs to recommend the Queen to send an Ambassador to the King of Denmark anent certain ships, merchandise, and persons detained wrongfully by the said King, and also anent certain "great and new tolls" imposed upon the merchants of Scotland desiring to import timber. The burghs again agreed to raise from themselves the necessary expenses.

The further steps in this negotiation are highly interesting, as showing the important position the Convention of Royal Burghs held then in the affairs of the nation. The resolution above alluded to was arrived at on the 24th February, 1563. On the next day the Queen declared her will that the Commissioners of the burghs should put in writing the names of certain "noble men" whom they thought fit and proper persons to go to the King of Denmark, to the number of ten or twelve, out of whom Her Majesty should choose one "and further declare her will." The Commissioners accordingly nominated the Lord Ruthven, the Lord of St. John, and Master John Hay, and sent in the names to the Queen the same day. On the 28th of February the Queen asked the Commissioners for the names of certain other persons over and above those first nominated. Accordingly, on that day the Commissioners added the names of the Lord Justice-Clerk, the Tutor of Petcur, the Laird of Whittinghame, and the Laird of Elphingston. Of these the Queen named, on the 4th of March, the Laird of Whittinghame, who was accordingly sent with a suite of eight persons, of whom two were to be merchants of good repute, and the burghs "stented"[50] themselves in the sum of twenty-eight hundred merks for their expenses.

The trade with France was threatened in 1570 with certain undesirable restrictions. It was reported in July of that year to the "Rycht Honorabil Provest" and Council of Edinburgh that the King of France had issued a proclamation (at the instigation of the Bishop of Glasgow) forbidding any Scottish merchants to trade with France, except they had the license of the Queen-Mother or her lieutenants. A certain Captain Ninian Cockburn declared to the Council of Edinburgh that he had good hopes of getting this proclamation rescinded; and the Council agreed, if he could manage this within three months, to pay him three hundred crowns of the sun, current money of France, or its equivalent in Scots money. This attempt was apparently not successful, for in October of the same year the Commissioners of the Royal Burghs agreed to send "one or two honest men, merchants," with writings under their common seal, to the King of France to try and induce him to withdraw the proclamation above referred to. Accordingly, Master Henry Nesbit, burgess and merchant of Edinburgh, was appointed to go to France, and the rest of the burghs agreed to repay him 15 shillings Scots for every franc he paid for his expenses.

At the same time the Commissioners ordained letters to be raised to bring home the Conservator in Flanders, that order might be taken concerning the Scottish merchants in that country. The condition of the Netherlands at this time was not favourable for commerce, and accordingly we find that in 1574 the burghs petitioned the Lord Regent to consent to the temporary change of the staple to Calais, "quhill it sall pleis God to bring the contry of Flanderis in quyetnes as it hes bene befoir," and to permit "ane qualefeit man of the merchant estait and nane other" to go to Calais and arrange matters. The Conservator in Flanders was also directed to appear at the next Convention.

Meantime the embassy to Denmark seems to have produced some result, for in the same year (1574) the King of Denmark agreed to admit the ships of the Scottish nation to all parts of his dominion provided they had the "coquet" of the port from whence they came.

The next Convention was held in 1575, and the Conservator of the Scottish trade in Flanders (Master George Halkett) duly appeared, and "lang resonyng vpon the troubilsum estait in Flanderis" took place. The result was that in the first place an increase of emoluments was voted unanimously to Master George for the two years following, and certain articles were formulated for the greater benefit and convenience of the Scottish traders. Very little good seems to have followed from this, for in 1577 a special commissioner, Master Nicholas Uddert, of Edinburgh, was directed to go to Flanders with letters from the Regent and the Convention, for the purpose of placing the staple in the most commodious place. He was to be accompanied by the Conservator (who seems to have remained in Scotland till then), and the additional fees authorized by the Act of 1575 were ordered to be paid for all time coming till the will of the Convention was further declared.

This arrangement only lasted for a very short time. The following year (1578) the Commissioners cancelled the bargain, and empowered Henry Nesbit, burgess of Edinburgh, as their Commissioner, to arrange with the town of Campvere for the transport of the Scottish staple to that place. The original commission and instructions to Nesbit are still preserved in the Records of the Convention of Royal Burghs. The first is a document of great importance as showing the position of the burghs at this time. It is addressed by the Provost, Bailies, and Council of Edinburgh to "the mighty and noble lordis, burghmasters, judges, and magistrates of the town of Campvere in Zealand;" and recites that the Commissioners of the burghs of Scotland having by the laws of Scotland and the privileges granted by their Kings the right as the "estate of merchants" to reason and decide in all matters concerning their common weal, had agreed to send Master Henry Nesbit to arrange for placing their common staple with them, as it had been in times of old.

The instructions desire that all the privileges and freedoms granted before by the Earls of Flanders, Dukes of Brabant, the Emperor Charles V. and his son should be anew approved, granted, and kept without violation or diminution. More particularly it is required that a deep and safe channel for the entry of the Scots ships into the harbour should be marked off; that berths at the quays should be reserved for them free of charge; that custom should only be paid once at an appointed place; that the factors' houses should be free from all imposts; that the judgment of all cases should be left to the Conservator; that "an honourable place" be appointed for preaching and praying according to the custom of the Scots nation; and that certain privileges should be procured from the town of Antwerp. Master George Halkett does not appear to have given unqualified satisfaction, for in 1581 the burghs desired that he should be discharged from his office, and ordered home to give an account of his doings.

The following year it was ordered by the Convention that no sailor should be employed in Scottish vessels except those certificated to be actual residents in free burghs and bearing charges there, under severe penalties. In 1582 the burghs agreed that no factor in Zealand, Holland, or Brabant should be permitted to act unless he was a professor of the true religion, and the same day the Convention, understanding that many of the merchants and traders resorting to France and Flanders had daily intercourse in the way of business with "ignorant and conjurit papists," whereby "great and abominable errors" might ensue, declared that no Scottish merchant should for the future have any manner of dealing with or "haunt or use the company of" any trader "nochtt of the trew religion," and every transgressor was to be fined £40. In spite of this prohibition the merchants appear not to have conducted themselves without reproach, as in 1586 the burghs heavily lamented their backslidings, and "thair vncumlie behaviour in thair eivill lyfe and outwarth manneris," and agreed forthwith to "erect ane Scottis kirk" in Campvere for remedy thereof, and in the following year they further agreed to appoint a minister for the church, who was to be paid by an additional duty on goods or by other methods suggested.

It would occupy too much space to continue in detail the history of the trade and commerce of Scotland during the sixteenth and seventeenth centuries. The object of these papers is not to give a complete account of early Scotland (which indeed would be impossible), but rather to indicate the sources from which such a history may in the future be compiled.

The full and admirable preface to the Ledger of Halyburton, printed in the series of Scottish Chronicles and Memorials, shows the transactions of a Scottish merchant during the Middle Ages, and is of the highest interest for this purpose. The preface, by the late Professor Cosmo Innes, gives an admirable account of the commerce of Scotland during the fifteenth and sixteenth centuries. The Records of the Convention of Royal Burghs supply details of the utmost importance for the period at which we have arrived.

Having dealt generally with the foreign trade of Scotland during the sixteenth century, during which, with some vicissitudes, it made remarkable progress, we come now to the seventeenth century, during which the principal new factor in the situation is the accession of the Sovereign of Scotland to the throne of England.

The first source of information is found in the Acts of the Parliament of Scotland.

By a statute of 1607 it was remitted to the burghs of Edinburgh, Perth, Dundee, Aberdeen, Glasgow, Ayr, St. Andrews, Montrose, Kirkcudbright, Irvine, Craile, Burntisland, and Culross to meet and set down order for furthering trade and navigation by reformation of abuses, and encouraging the building of "great ships."

Some time after this, great damage was caused to Scottish shipping by the pirates of Dunkirk, and in 1630 the burghs gave in an article to Parliament on the subject. The Estates agreed to petition the King to consider the deplorable state of the merchants, and to provide some means by which they might be protected in their peaceable trading. In 1645 the Earls of Tullibardine, Southesk, and Lanark, the Lairds of Manor Dawick and Udny and the Commissioners for Edinburgh, Aberdeen,

K

and Irvine, were appointed a committee to consider the question of the India trade.

The same year one John Cartwright supplicated Parliament that he might be made a free citizen of the kingdom, and that he might have in his commerce with the East Indies the same privileges which the King of Denmark offered for a similar traffic.

Towards the close of the century, in 1695, there was passed the famous Act for establishing a company for trading to Africa and the Indies.

A very good general idea of the commercial state of Scotland in the middle of the seventeenth century will be found in the report presented to the Commissioners for Appeals in 1656 by Mr. Tucker, who was sent down specially to inquire into the excise and customs. His report contains many curious particulars bearing on foreign trade, and shows conclusively the commercial decay which had taken place.

"Although," he says, "Scotland is almost encompassed with the sea (which hath very many inletts into the mayneland), and hath a very greate number of islands adjoyneing thereunto, both on the easterne and westerne parts thereof, and soe naturally comodious for commerce and traffique, yett the barrenesse of the countrey, poverty of the people, generally affected with slothe, and a lazy vagrancy of attending and followeing theyr heards up and downe in theyr pastorage, rather than any dextrous improvement of theyr time, hath quite banished all trade from the inland parts, and drove her downe to the very sea side, where that little which is still remayneing (and was never greate in the most proude and flourishing times) lives, pent and shutt up in a very small compasse, even of those parts where there is any exercised, which is mostly and chiefly on the east part, and soe northerly along the side of the German Ocean, or else on the westerne part, along Dunbryton Fyrth into the Irish or English Seas, the rest of the country from that Fyrth on the west side with all the islands up towards the most northerne headland, being inhabited by the old Scotts or wilde Irish, and speakeing theyr language, which live by feeding cattle up and downe the hills, or else fishing and fowleing and formerly (till that they have of late been restrayned) by plaine downright robbing and stealeing."

He then goes on to describe the eight "most eminent places of Trade," which were, on the East Sea, Leith, Bo'ness, Burntisland, Dundee, Aberdeen, and Inverness; and, on the West Sea, Glasgow and Ayr. These ports included certain other smaller places in their immediate neighbourhood. The chief port of Scotland then for foreign trade was Leith. Next in importance came Bo'ness, which had a large commerce in coal and salt chiefly carried on in Dutch vessels to the Low Countries. Burntisland, with its dependent harbours on the north side of the Forth, had a small trade outwards with coal and salt, and inwards from Norway for timber, and with France for wines. The whole combined shipping of the ports on the north side of the Forth numbered only fifty vessels, of which the largest was 100 tons burden.

Tucker does not hesitate to speak plainly. Mentioning Dundee, he describes it as "sometime a towne of riches and trade, but the many *rencontres* it hath mett with all in the time of domestick comotions, and her obstinacy and pride of late yeares rendring her a prey to the soldier, have much shaken and abated her former grandeur; and, notwithstanding all, she remaynes still, though not glorious, yett not contemptible." Dundee and Aberdeen were the principal seats of the fishing exports, and also had a fair trade with Norway, Holland, and France. Some little business was also done exporting the homespun plaiding. The combined shipping of Dundee and Montrose amounted to 22 vessels, of which the two largest were 120 tons burden each; and Aberdeen owned nine vessels.

The Western commerce was very much the same. Glasgow did a small trade with Ireland in coal in open boats of from four to ten tons burden, bringing back butter, meal, oats, hoops, and barrel staves; with France, exporting herrings, plaiding, and coals, and importing salt, pepper, rosin, and prunes; with Norway for timber, and formerly some went as far as Barbadoes. Glasgow possessed 12 vessels, of which no fewer than three were each of 150 tons burden, being apparently the largest vessels owned in Scotland at the time (1656).

The last document which we shall quote on this subject is a report which was made to the Convention of Royal Burghs on the state and condition of the principal towns in Scotland in 1692. From this it appears that the merchants of Edinburgh owned 13 ships, the largest of which was 150 tons burden, and 17 "barks," the largest of which was 40 tons burden. During the year preceding five of the 13 ships made each two voyages to Holland with cargoes of coal, wood, lead ore, and sheep skins. One went to Bilbao, but had not then returned. The others traded to Hamburg, Amsterdam, and London with varied cargoes. All the barks were for the coasting trade except two, which had gone to the Sound with herring. Dundee had one ship of 200 tons, and about 14 others smaller. Glasgow valued her foreign trade at £205,000 (Scots), and had eight ships then at home, belonging to merchants of the town, and seven away on voyages. The largest of the fleet was the *James*, belonging to George Lockhart, of 160 tons burden, and valued at £6,000 (Scots).

The town of Ayr had no ships, barks, or boats, "save a little boat of the value of £40 (Scots) belonging to John Campbell." The foreign trade of Ayr for the preceding five years was as follows, viz. :—Four-fifths of the cargo of a small vessel from Virginia of 70 tons burden; three small vessels coming from Stockholm with iron; 20 lasts of tar and some few deals from Norway; about 20 tons of French wine; 16 casks of Canary, and a small vessel from the West Indies with sugar.

CHAPTER VIII.

WEIGHTS AND MEASURES.

The subject of the early weights and measures is one of considerable importance for historical students, and at the same time it is one of very great practical difficulty. Almost every county and district had its own customary measures, which differed from the national standards and also from one another. This confusion no doubt originally arose from historical causes; and it continued, in spite of every effort made by Parliament and by the Convention of Royal Burghs, which was really the body which dealt principally with commercial matters, down to the close of the last century.

In dealing with the subject the most convenient way will be to give in the first place a very brief view of the history of the system of weights and measures as a whole.

The first recorded Act is the Assize of Measures

and Weights, which is usually attributed to David I. There can be little doubt but that this, or some similar regulation, is really due to that king, though the actual date of the earliest existing MS. of the laws belongs to the period of Robert the Bruce. In 1365 the chamberlain was ordered to see that a "tron," or weighing machine, was erected in every port in the kingdom, and that the bailies of burghs examined regularly the weights and measures, and punished those who were guilty of offences against the regulations.

The next important Act on the subject occurs in 1425, when the Parliament of James I. issued a series of orders relating to the various measures, and requiring standards to be made and issued from Edinburgh. In 1457 the size of the pint, firlot, half firlot, and peck were fixed, and standards were to be kept in Edinburgh, Perth, and Aberdeen.

Ten years later, in 1467, another Act required all weights and measures throughout the country to be reformed, and the chamberlains and sheriffs were enjoined to see that the provisions of the Act were enforced. In 1503 weights and measures were again ordered to be of the standards to be fixed by the king and his chamberlain; each burgh was to have a sealed measure, and any one using other than the new standards were to be indicted. No burgh was to have one set of weights for buying and another for selling.

The water measure in use and wont throughout the country was still to be preserved by Acts of 1555 and 1567; but the latter Act provided for a "straik" measure, without prejudice to the water mett.

An important enactment was made in 1597, which altered the old standard of the firlot as fixed in 1457, making it larger, and declaring that in future victual was to be measured by "straik" instead of heap.

The last important Act was passed in 1618, following on the appointment of a Commission of Enquiry. This Act entered very minutely into all the weights and measures, and fixed the standards which practically remained in use up to the time of the Union.

In spite, however, of all these Parliamentary regulations it is certain that great irregularity prevailed throughout the country; and the subject was very frequently brought under the notice of the Convention of Burghs. In 1552 the provosts and commissioners of burghs assembled at Edinburgh resolved that the whole burghs of the kingdom should receive their measures from the standards following, viz., the stone weight of Lanark, the pint of Stirling, the firlot of Linlithgow, and the ell of Edinburgh. In 1578 the Convention decided that the pound should contain sixteen ounces of the French weight, and that every burgh should have a stone weight, half stone weight, pound, and half pound, made of brass, marked with the stamp of the town using them; and that the firlots should conform to the Linlithgow standard and be similarly marked. The commissioner from Glasgow wished, in 1579, an Act of Parliament to be passed making "straik" measure legal instead of heaped. Uniformity in weights and measures was again strenuously enjoined in 1587, with special reference to the Act of Convention of 1552. Every burgh not providing weights was to be fined; and in 1594 a return was required from each, showing that they had complied with the Act. In the same year Linlithgow was ordered to furnish to each municipality requiring it a firlot measure with two bands and a cross band on the bottom, of iron, with a peck and a half peck measure—all for six pounds Scots. At the next Convention, in 1595, the commissioners of Wigton, Kirkcudbright, Dumfries, and Jedburgh declared that the ancient measures in their districts were larger than the Linlithgow standard, and great difficulty would be found in altering them. The matter came up again in the Convention next year, and it was decided that four pecks, neither more nor less, should go to the firlot of Linlithgow, and that this decision should be binding on all the country, except in Nithsdale, where the customary old measure was allowed to be used.

The same Convention also agreed that the water measure of victual and salt imported from foreign countries should contain eighteen pecks to the boll, and be divided into boll, half boll, and quarter boll, and be used by all burghs under pecuniary penalties. All native goods were to be received, sold, and delivered according to the stone weight of Lanark and its pound and half pound, but foreign goods were to be weighed according to the Mint weight of sixteen ounces to the pound. The ell was to be in every case the ell of Edinburgh.

The western burghs, and especially Ayr, Irvine, and Dumbarton, had customary measures, which were apparently larger than those used in other parts of the country. Various complaints were made about these, and in 1602, at the Convention held at Ayr in July, the provost and bailies of that burgh were ordered to have their quart, pint, choppin, and mutchkin conform to the stoup of Stirling.

At Haddington, in 1603, the town of Wigton was ordered to choose common measurers, who were to be responsible for measuring truly all sorts of cloth; but, having failed to do this, the matter was reported to the Convention at Perth in 1604, and the burgh was fined £20 for non-compliance with the order, and again ordained to appoint measurers. This matter came up once more at Dumfries in 1605, when it was decided that buyers and sellers of cloth should be free to arrange with one another for the measuring of cloth, but in case of dispute a reference was to be made to the common measurer, and the seller was to pay him a fee of ten pennies.

The burgh of Glasgow was ordered in 1607 to conform their tron weight to the standard of Lanark, and their troy weights to those of France.

The Convention of Royal Burghs after the Act of Parliament of 1618 made frequent attempts from time to time to secure the much to be desired uniformity in the standards. Thus in 1689 among the grievances of the Burghs formally enumerated for the favourable consideration of Parliament, the twenty-third item was that "redres be craved of the great grievance of the inequality of measurs that are within royall burghs and burghs of barronie and regalitie such as Dalkeith and vthers and that the Act of Parliament 1587 anent mets and measures be revived."

At the Union the Imperial standards superseded formally the ancient system, though for long afterwards and down to the beginning of the present century custom proved stronger than law.

At a very early period, and certainly before 1552, the standards of the ell, the stone, the stoup or pint, and the firlot, were entrusted to the keeping of the burghs of Edinburgh, Lanark, Stirling, and Linlithgow respectively. It will now be convenient to consider the history of each of these.

The unit of lineal measure in mediæval Scotland appears to have been the "eln" or ell. The "Burgh Laws" ordain that every burgess is to have in his house a "mesure to met his corne, *ane elnewand*, a stane and punde wecht for til wey": and in the "Assize of Kyng Dauid of Mesuris and Wechtis" the first article treats "of the eln."

The Scottish ell contained thirty-seven inches, each inch being equal in length to three selected barley or bere corns without their tails (*sine caudis*); or to the length of the thumb of a man of middle stature, measuring to the root of the nail (*pollex autem debet mensurari ad radicem unguis pollicis*).

The assize of James I. in 1425 confirmed the statute of David I. "ande deliverit the elne to contene xxxvij inches."

The Commission appointed in 1587 to consider and settle the standards for the whole country declared that the ell measure of Edinburgh containing thirty-seven inches was to be the standard of length. In 1617 the Commissioners, then appointed, confirmed and ratified the findings of their predecessors so far as the ell was concerned, and ordered the standard of the ell measure to be kept by the burgh of Edinburgh. The foot measure came into use shortly afterwards, and is first mentioned in the parliamentary records in 1663. An Act of that year provides that for the future the foot is to consist of twelve inches, each equal to one thirty-seventh part of the standard ell measure of Edinburgh. It appears that the ell had been divided erroneously into forty-two inches, and a customary foot of twelve of these shorter inches had come into common use. The Act orders a standard foot of iron or copper to be provided by the Magistrates of Edinburgh before 1st January, 1664, and all burghs before the 1st of March of the same year were ordained to have measures made from it and hung on their tolbooth doors or market crosses, by which all wrights, glaziers, masons, and other workmen were to work.

In 1685 the Parliament of James VII. declared that three barley corns set lengthways should make one inch; that twelve inches should make one foot; that three feet should make one yard; that three feet and one inch should make one ell; and that one thousand seven hundred and sixty yards should make one mile; and this was to be the standard in computing distances from place to place in all time coming.

The standard of the "eln" was of old committed

Standards of the Ell in the Custody of the City of Edinburgh :—

Fig. 1.—Imperial Yard and English Ell (= 45 inches), 1707.
Fig. 2.—Ancient Scottish Ell Standard, of Iron, = 37 inches.
Fig. 3.—Scottish Ell, 1663, = 37 inches.

to the custody of the city of Edinburgh; and the Corporation has still an ancient iron measure, long popularly known as the elnwand or ellbed, which seems to have originally been suspended on the wall of the Council Chamber or Tolbooth. It measures 37·001 inches imperial, but the marks and stamps on it are now so much rusted they are illegible. The city has also a standard copper ell measure, made in pursuance of the Act of 1663. These standards, and the Imperial one sent in 1707, are engraved in the accompanying plate.

The unit of weight was originally the wheat corn. In the "Assisa de Mensuris et Ponderibus" it is mentioned that the sterling or silver penny in the time of King David weighed thirty-two corns of good and round wheat. The ounce at the same period was equal to twenty sterlings or 640 grains of wheat; and the pound weighed twenty-five shillings, or three hundred sterlings, or 9600 grains, and was divided into fifteen ounces. The stone for weighing wool and other gear of this period weighed fifteen pounds, but the stone of wax only eight pounds. The "waw" contained twelve stones.

The Parliament of 1425 ordained that the stone should weigh fifteen Troy pounds, and should be divided into sixteen Scots pounds. But in the

Assize of Weights and Measures made at Perth in the reign of James I., the stone to weigh iron, wool, and other merchandise was ordered to contain sixteen pounds Troy, and each pound sixteen ounces Troy,. and these weights remained the same till the Union.

In Hunter's Treatise of Weights, Metts, and Measures of Scotland, printed in 1624, the system of Scottish weights in his time is thus laid down. A pickle of wheat taken out of the middle of the ear is the foundation of a grain weight. Thirty-six grains make a drop weight; sixteen drops make an ounce; eight ounces equal a mark; two marks go to a pound; and sixteen of these pounds are contained in the stone weight of Lanark.

The tron stone weight contained nineteen pounds eight ounces of the weights of the Paris standard, and was used for butter, cheese, tallow, and such like country commodities. Tron weight was abolished by the act of 1618, but continued in use for long afterwards.

The light ton which was in use at the beginning of the seventeenth century for weighing goods between Scotland and France, England and Spain, weighed six hundred pounds.

Merchandise between Scotland and the Low Countries at the same period was measured by the sack, which weighed six hundred and forty pounds Scots.

Trade between Scotland and the Eastern Countries was measured by the serplath of 1280 pounds Scots. The last was equal to 1920 lbs. Scots, but varied greatly, in some cases being equal to 4000 lbs. A last of wool was held equal to twelve sacks, or for ship measure ten sacks. A last of hides was twenty dakers, or 200 skins. As a liquid measure the last of beer was equal to twelve barrels. The "fiddes," used only for lead, contained one hundred and twenty stones.

The standard stone, which was ordered in 1618 to be kept by the Burgh of Lanark, is not now there. But a stone weight with the arms of Lanark is in the custody of the City of Edinburgh, and it is probable that this is the original standard. The other weights of the series were 8 pounds, 4 pounds, 2 pounds and 1 pound respectively; and in the Edinburgh set the 1 pound is marked as equal to 7,620 grains English.

The first liquid measure noted in the Scots Acts is the gallon, which is mentioned in the "Assisa Regis David." It was ordained to be $6\frac{1}{2}$ inches deep, $8\frac{1}{2}$ inches in diameter, 27 inches in circumference at the top, and 23 inches in circumference at the bottom, and to contain 4 pounds weight each of standing, running, and salt water, or 12 pounds weight in all. Another gallon in use, in the time of David I., contained only 10 pounds 4 ounces of water, but the distinction in their use is not given. The pint is mentioned in the Act of 1425, and is required to contain 41 ounces of clear water of Tay, equal to 2 pounds 9 ounces Troy weight. In 1457, the pint of Stirling is mentioned as having been given into the custody of that burgh, by order of the three estates, at the time that Sir John Forester was Chamberlain (1425-1448); and it is ordained to be the universal standard throughout all the country. By this Act, the gallon was to weigh 20 pounds 8 ounces. The Commissioners appointed to regulate measures and weights in 1617 found that the Stirling pint contained 3 pounds 7 ounces Troy of clear running water, of the water of Leith. The Stirling Pint Jug is still preserved, and the engraving (Frontispiece Fig. 1) is a correct representation of it.

From a report made in 1827 the following particulars are taken.

The jug is described as being in the form of the frustum of a cone, the diameter of the bottom being $5\frac{1}{10}$ inches, that of the mouth $4\frac{1}{10}$ inches, and the depth 6 inches. It is composed of a kind of brass, and from its rude construction has evidently been fabricated at a period when the arts had made little progress in Scotland. It bears upon its side in bold relief the figure of a lion rampant; and another object which has been variously described as a child in a recumbent position, and also the wolf in the arms of Stirling, though it is more likely to be meant for the latter, from the fact that a standard pint in the custody of the City of Edinburgh bears the Stirling arms in the same place. When the jug was filled with distilled water at a temperature of 62° of Fahrenheit, the contents weighed 26,286·41 grains imperial, the barometer being at 30 inches.

Eight pints of the Stirling standard made one gallon Scots measure, which, according to the above report, should contain 210,291·28 imperial grains; and bear to the imperial gallon the proportion of 3·004161 to unity.

Each pint was divided into two choppins, and each choppin into two mutchkins. In the valuable collection of ancient standards, preserved by the corporation of Edinburgh, there is a choppin measure with the date 1555 between the arms of Scotland, and those of the City of Edinburgh. (See Frontispiece Fig. 2.)

The old Scottish dry measures are noticed first in the "Assisa de Ponderibus," where the boll is to be 9 inches deep and 24 inches in diameter, and to contain 12 gallons of ale. The Parliament of 1425 ordered standard measures of the boll, firlot, half firlot, peck and gallon to be issued at Edinburgh, which were to come into use on the 1st of September following. From the "Assize of Weights and Measures" of the same year, it would appear that a completely new system was then introduced. The boll is ordained to contain 4 firlots, and these firlots seem to be of a different size from those then in use or from those of an earlier date. Each firlot was to contain 41 pounds weight of clear water of Tay and each boll 164 pounds. This was 41 pounds heavier than the earlier boll of King David, which contained 123 pounds weight of various kinds of water.

In 1457 the firlot was ordered to contain 18 pints of the Stirling stoup, and three new standards of the pint and firlot were to be made and one sent to Aberdeen, one to Perth, and one to Edinburgh. These measures remained in force till the Commission of 1587, when the Commissioners discovered that an error had been made in 1457 with regard to the contents of the firlot, which should contain 19 pints and a "jowcat" or gill. The error is said to have arisen "be errour of the prentair." In future "victual" measure is to be "straik," not "heaped." But because it was in use to estimate malt, bear, and oats by heaped measure, or one third more than the straik, the Commissioners remitted to the Privy Council to consider whether a new measure should not be adopted for these articles, or whether the same standard should be in use for them as for wheat, rye, beans, peas, meal and white salt, which were sold by straik, only giving three for two or six for four. Accordingly, the Lords of the Privy Council decided that the firlot should be $18\frac{1}{6}$ inches wide and $7\frac{1}{2}$ inches deep, and should contain 19 pints and 2 "jowcats," and be used for all articles sold by "straik" measure, and that one third more be given for those sold by heaped measure. Minute directions were also laid down for the manufacture of the standards, of which a double set were to be made, and one kept in the Register in Edinburgh and the other committed to the custody of the burghs to which they had been committed of old.

Notwithstanding these regulations great complaints still continued about the diversity of weights and measures, and the Commission of 1618 summoned the Provost and Bailies of Linlithgow to appear before them and produce the standard firlot. On their appearance the Commissioners tested the firlot and found that it contained 21 pints and a "mutchkin" (equal to about an English pint). The Provost and Bailies were solemnly sworn and deponed that the said measure was the one which had been in use for the last fifty or sixty years; and that "the most ancient and aged persons in their burgh" had never known or heard of any other. The standard was then measured and found to be 19⅚ inches in width and 7⅓ inches in depth, showing a very considerable difference from the standard of 1587, which is never alluded to in the proceedings and seems to have been quite ignored both by the corporation and "the most ancient and aged persons" of the burgh.

After full consideration the Commissioners decided that this was to be the standard in all time coming; and to be marked with four crowns on the bottom and five impressions of the letter L on the lip. They also found that the difference between the "straik" and heaped measure of this firlot was not a third part, and that great injustice was done by the custom of giving three for two, which had been in common use. Accordingly, they ordered a new standard firlot to be made for malt, bear, and oats, to contain 31 pints of the Stirling jug, and to be 19⅚ inches in width and 10½ inches in depth. These standards were to have one more iron band round them and to be marked with the letter H on the outside. Four of either of these firlots were to make a just boll.

In 1624 the dry measures were four lippies or forpits to the peck, four pecks to the firlot, four firlots to the boll or bow, and sixteen bowes to the chalder. The firlot of the straik measure was equal to ·99825 of an imperial bushel; and the heaped corn firlot, to 1·45627 imperial bushel. The standard firlot committed of old to the custody of the Burgh of Linlithgow is not now extant. It unfortunately perished in a fire in the Town House in 1847.

The following table shows the imperial equivalents of the old customary measure of the boll which was in use in Scotland up to the year 1827, and which is not altogether even now extinct.

	HEAPED.			STRAIK.		
	B.	Pk.	Galls.	B.	Pk.	Galls.
Aberdeen,	6	1	1·544	4	3	1·416
Argyll, Inveraray,	6	1	0·411			
„ Achnabreck,	6	2	0·426			
„ Cantire,	7	3	1·014			
Ayr,	7	3	0·045	3	3	1·022
Banff,	6	1	0·256	4	1	0·551
Berwick,	5	3	0·667	3	3	1·111
Bute,	7	3	0·759	3	3	1·379
Caithness,	6	1	0·566			
Clackmannan,	6	0	1·418			
Dumbarton,	6	1	1·019	3	3	1·943
Elgin and Moray,	6	0	1·006	4	0	1·691
Fife,	5	3	0·957	4	0	0·188

	Heaped.			Straik.		
	B.	Pk.	Galls.	B.	Pk.	Galls.
Forfar, Dundee, - - -	5	3	1.353	4	0	0.320
,, other places, - -	6	0	0.104	4	0	1.072
Inverness, - - - - -	6	0	0.917	4	0	0.484
Kincardine, N. part, - -	6	1	1.544	3	3	1.944
,, S. part, - -	6	0	0.104	4	0	1.072
Kinross, - - - - - -	5	3	0.565	3	3	1.919
Kircudbright—						
,, bet. Orr & Fleet,	10	2	1.311			
,, West of Fleet, -	11	2	1.067			
,, East of Orr, -	9	2	1.556			
*Linlithgow, (Stand.) -	5	3	0.601	3	3	1.944
Nairn, { Barley, - - -	6	0	1.097	} 4	2	0.823
{ Oats, - - - -	7	2	1.371			
Renfrew, - - - - - -	6	1	0.445	3	3	1.944
Ross and Cromarty, - -	5	3	1.735	3	3	1.699
Roxburgh, - - - - -	6	0	0.442	6	0	0.442
,, Teviotdale, - -	7	2	0.552	5	0	1.508
Selkirk, - - - - - -	7	1	1.274	4	3	0.765
Stirling, - - - - - -	6	0	1.181	3	3	1.919
Sutherland, - - -	6	0	0.102	3	3	1.944

The ancient land measures of Scotland are exceedingly complicated, and different systems prevailed for long in various parts of the country. The earliest legislative enactment which has been preserved is contained in the collected "Fragments," printed in the first volume of the Record Edition of the Scots Acts. It provides that the rood of land in baronies is to contain six ells or eighteen feet of a medium-sized man; and that the rood of land in burghs is to contain twenty feet. The fall is to contain six ells; the rood, forty falls; the acre,

* The Linlithgow measures were used in the other counties.

four roods; the oxgang, thirteen acres, and the plough-land, eight oxgangs.

These measures continued without any practical alteration to the Union; and are thus explained in the *Treatise on the Weights and Measures of Scotland*, printed in 1624. Six ells of the standard of Edinburgh make a lineal fall; six ells long by six broad make a square fall; forty square falls make a rood, whether ten by four or eight by five. The acre is equal to 160 falls or 960 ells. Four acres are counted for a minister's glebe, and four oxgangs equal a pound land of old extent. The rood of land contains 240 ells; but the rood of mason's work contains only 36 ells.

In those parts of Scotland which were latest in forming part of the ancient kingdom various systems of land measurement, more or less exact, long continued customary. In the north-eastern part of the country the "davach" was a common measure, and extended to four plough-lands, or as much ground as four ploughs could till in a season. In Orkney the lands were estimated by ounce lands, each made up of eighteen penny lands. A mark-land in Orkney was about $1\frac{1}{4}$ acre. The penny lands varied in extent very considerably. Capt. Thomas, in an interesting article in the *Proceedings of the Society of Antiquaries of Scotland*, estimates the average size of the penny-land as being about eight or nine acres; but all these were rather measures of produce than of surface. The "plank" of land, however, was generally the same in extent throughout Orkney, and contained $1\frac{1}{9}$ acre Scots or 1·32 acre English.

The important fishing industry had a special series of measures which underwent the usual changes. Aberdeen is the earliest place which is mentioned as having a standard for fish. In 1478 it was ordered that salmon be packed in barrels of the measure of Hamburgh and the Assize of Aberdeen, and in 1487 the barrel is defined as containing 14 gallons. In 1540 the system of branding the barrels was ordained to be in force. Every cooper was to have a branding iron with a distinguishing mark, and each burgh was also to put a mark on the barrels, guaranteeing the amount. Failure to comply with these provisions was followed by forfeiture, one half to the crown and the other to the town. The standard for salmon was to be kept at Aberdeen; and that for herrings and white fish at Edinburgh, and each of the burghs was to have duplicates. In 1570 the salmon barrel was said to contain 12 gallons, and that for white fish and herrings 10 gallons, but the Act of 1581 orders the herring barrel to contain 9 gallons. Different measures seem to have been in use in the west country. For in 1595 the burghs assembled at Glasgow, and reduced the hogshead of fish from 18 gallons to 14½, and the barrel to one half the hogshead.

In 1641 complaints were made abroad about both the quantity and the quality of the salmon exported, to the discredit of the native merchants and the dishonour of the nation ; wherefore Parliament enacted that all and sundry acts, laws and constitutions of the country made anent the salmon trade should be ratified and approved, with this addition, that all the coopers in the kingdom were to make the barrels of good and sufficient Baltic oak, without worm holes or white wood, and of sufficient strength and tightness to bear handling and retain the pickle. The barrels were to contain ten gallons of the Stirling pint, conform to an Act of Privy Council in 1619, and to be branded as formerly.

The barrel of green fish was to contain 12 gallons. In the Forth, herrings were measured by a standard called the "two hundred herring mett," which contained 42 Stirling pints.

Stirling Standard Jug preserved by the City of Edinburgh.

APPENDIX.

EXTRACT FROM THE *Ulster Journal of Archæology*, SHOW-
ING THE TRIBAL CASUALTIES OF THE CELTIC
PERIOD IN IRELAND.

THE "*croes*," or herds, of various species, formed with the herdsmen a *creaght*, which moved along the hills and through the woods, rendering, as a seignioral due, either one of each species of "*Cro*," or sometimes, on the death of their "can-finny"[1] (ceann finè, or head of the kin owning the stock), the best as a *heriot;* or else a few pence per head. As among the Germans, no limit of space was assigned to the occupancy. Tyrone did not "sett any portion of land"; and his receipts of chief-rent were therefore uncertain, because the *can-finnys*, as "free tenants," could, "by the custom of the country," remove from under "one lord to another."

The "certayne custome" above alluded to, of rendering victual, had many ramifications, a few of which may be noticed. The Gaelic military force, whose *status* is well expressed in ancient ballads by the designation of "the Kempery men," or men of the camp, were, with their *taoiseach*, or leader, supported throughout the country by the *creaghts*—a practice used by the Earl of Tyrone as lately as the 17th century.[2] The primary "rent" to the king (of which presently) and other charges, some of which also became a species of rent, arose from this nomad mode

[1] *Pat. Jac.* I. [2] *Arch. Tracts*, II. 30.

of maintenance. During peace, as Davyes observed, the chief of Feara-managh asked no more than he was entitled to :—" But in time of war," wrote Sir John, " marry! he made himself owner of all " ; taxing as he listed, and imposing as many *bonaghts,* or hired soldiers, as he had occasion to use." The king was then justly empowered to exert every means, and raise the sinews of defensive war by an impost which was not for his own particular benefit, and the very name of which, *bon-caght,* signifies the original payment rendered by maintaining the military.

To sustain armed defenders was with clansmen the next duty to that of rising at the *gairm sluaigh;* and accordingly follows it in a list of "duties and rents" to M'Carthy More, being the custom of rendering to the chief and his men two principal articles of Irish sustenance, namely, oatmeal and butter, which, as the custom had now become " certayne," were given by measure, and therefore termed *sorren.* Bonaght, or the primary charge of maintaining soldiery, was specially due on land modernly held by *sorren* tenure ;[1] and this *sorren* seems to have been the *coigne-bon,*[2] or refection originally given them ; being, as the record states, " otherwise *coigne,* as extorted by the Earl of Desmond, who was supposed to have invented this exaction, which he but adopted from the Irish." Originally it was merely "a nights meal" upon the land where " the Earl passed through with his forces " ; that is, on which the troop encamped. But as such a tax was uncertain, it was unequal ; and therefore *sorren more,* if the chief "did not come in place to spend it," became a "rent." For every parcel of land was " charged with its own portion time out of mind," having been commuted, from an unlimited refection, into a measure, or "*sroan,*" namely, "a gallon and a half of oatmeal flour made of burnt oats, and a *quirren*

---

[1] 1587, S.P.O. "*Desmond's Rents*" and *Ware,* I. 74.
[2] S.P. II. 502.

pottle, or 10 lbs. of butter, valued in times past—the one at 4d., and the other a groat"; and every parcel of sorren land sent certain numbers of these measures to the earl's residence. The earl also received his sorren from junior chiefs, such as O'Donoughue, O'Callaghan, etc., and from a priory whence it was due, either in kind or (at the prior's and "deputy-captayne's" choice) in money, each chief rent being valued at £4 8s. 8d. While some districts paid this rent, other *ceann-cinès* and monasteries were "charged with the higher tenure"[1] of receiving the chief and his train at *cuid-oidche*, or supper, equivalent to the modern dinner. The explanatory term for this provision, namely, "a portion, a meal, or a refection"[2] (*cuid* is a part or share), seems to denote the chief's gavel right to a *coigne*, or meal, as his partakeable portion of the fruits of the land. It seems also that the original method by which the nomad *Ri* was maintained was by these visitations, which came as such to be called "cosherie," possibly derived from *cios-ri*, namely, cess or rent for the king. This primitive mode of a chieftain maintaining his train in the houses of his clansmen (against which the very first printed statute, *anno* 1310, and another Act of 1634, were specially directed) was revived after the confiscations of the 17th century, when some of the kindliest feelings of human nature conspired to renew this ancient custom in order to support the families of fallen chiefs. The antiquity of the practice is, of course, greater than any native records, which, however, refer to it in deeds as early in date as the 11th century, when a certain petty king in Meath relinquished the right of having a night's *coinme* every quarter of a year at the tenement of a herenagh at Ardbracan,[3] and the king of Leinster released certain land "*a procuracione et expedicione mea*"—the former term implying provision for himself, and the latter, military

---

[1] Sir W. St. Leger, 1589, S.P.O. [2] *Carew MS.* 626.
[3] *Arch. Misc.* I. 143.

service and the charge of *bonaght*.¹ These two charges were evidently the fundamental imposts on land. There was also an offering called in Latin *satellitum poturæ*, drink for the king and his retinue, the exaction of which is alluded to in an ancient grant to an abbey.² When, in 1535, O'Neill renounced "refectiones vel expenses, quæ dicuntur proprie coyne, livery, coydeis, vel talia proculenta" (drinkings) "inter Anglicos,"³ he, in effect, promised to relieve the subjected Englishry from expending them by cosherie. The Latin word *expenses* is of course a translation of the English term for the outlay made in the reception of a chief and his retinue by the Irish tenantry, who even in the 17th century continued the ancient communistic custom of yielding convivial refections, or "common spendings" instead of paying rent; a practice vindicated by Spenser, and which was at first a payment for what was actually rented from the king and his troops, namely, protection. It was the most popular eulogium of any chieftain to declare him the spender and defender of his clan.

Modern great lords often feast their tenantry on the rent day, and their incomes are derived from vast earldoms that belonged to their ancestors in times when the Gaelic *seigneur* received no more than his share in the feast, which, with his lodging, was termed *cuid-oidche*, originally called a supper, but literally a "portion for one night." In the same manner this refection was at first the *coinme* and sole wages of the military; and it would seem that *caught*,⁴ a supper, is the origin of *cacht*, payment. *Buannacht bona*, *i.e.* the primary renderings, became "customary services";⁵ and the first usage, that of giving *sorren*, grew in course of time into the formal payment of rent.

In the 17th century *sorren* continued to be the head-rent of West Connaught, each quarter of land paying yearly

¹ *Regist. of All Hallows*, 50, 126. ² *Harris' Ware*, I. 75.
³ S.P. II. ⁴ Act of 1634. ⁵ *Four Masters*, p. 1601.

certain measures of meal—"Hibernicè vocatos *sruans*, cum sufficiente butiro." This was the "greddan meal and butter," said to have been presented in 1603 to O'Neill of Castlereagh by his servants, and which *Anglicè* was "strowan"— see *Ulster Journal of Archæology*, vol. III., p. 134; and p. 160, showing that oatmeal was part of the feudal rent of Ulster in the 13th century; also vol. II., p. 139, that "corn and butter" was the principal living of O'Neill and his clan. "Sorren land," probably for most part arable, designated a freehold, liable to this rendering; as "mart land," mostly pasture, may have been one whence a *mart* (the term still known in Scotland for a "beef," or salted cow) was to be sent in, for (as Sir John O'Reilly expressed it) "the spending of his house."[1] In Ophaly every ploughland rendered 24 sieves of oats, value 5s., and two beeves, 4s. 2d., to O'Conor, besides being liable to "taxes and customs."[2] This was *anno* 1550; and a rent so unusually regular was probably a composition arranged at the time when Henry VIII. was to have created the ruling chieftain a viscount. *Sorren* and *mart*, or meal and salted butter and beef, were the secondary form in which receipts from land accrued to the chieftain; who, in early ages, as has been seen, was interdicted from possessing anything, though all belonging to the clan was freely at his service: "of their own accord they gave him so many cattle, or a certain portion of grain"[3]—rude offerings subsequently made more acceptable by preparation for use; and these are apparently typified in the ceremony used in inaugurating a "public officer,"[4] and especially the king, of throwing wheat and salt over him as symbols that the plentifulness of peace should attend his reign.[5] Another ceremony of more antique times, that of the chief-elect and his clan eating of the same meat and drinking from the same vessel,

[1] *Carew MS.* 614.   [2] S.P.O. 1550.   [3] Logan's *Gael*, i. 171.
[4] *Camden*, 469.   [5] *Pac. Heb.* I. 163.

marked the community of property in food; and their quality was further insisted on by denying to the chief the use of any "cuppe or dish."[1] These at least seem to be the meaning of parts of an installatory ceremonial which was evidently misrepresented to Giraldus Cambrensis.

Equality of rank was strangely mingled with individual power in the position of the chieftain. To wear a similar garb, and to live sociably and on equal terms with the clansmen, secured to him their hearts. At court, Tyrone was an earl; yet, when there, he declared he would rather be "O'Neill" than Philip of Spain; but among the "Cinel Eoghain" he was merely the first of themselves, and, living among them in their simplicity of life, often received his "king's rent" as "cosherie" in their dwellings; or the feast was in the open air, where he held his court, and the brehons gave judgment; and, when seated among his clan "on a green bank," he was (as a contemporary observed) "in his greatest majesty.[2]

Penalties conceded to the king as the enforcer of càins, or legal fines, were probably his earliest receipts by right. The first mentioned in a list of dues to the chief of West Connaught, in the 17th century, is a sevenfold fine in every species of cattle for "stealths," which some Anglo-Irish lords endeavoured to prevent by fining the suffering tenant for his want of vigilance.[3] A portion of every *eric* was (like the Saxon *wite*), due to the chief for the homicide of men under his *comeric* or protection. O'Doyne paid a third of all càins, casualties, etc., arising in his country to a potent neighbour, O'Conor, for his *comeric*.[4] All who were under the rule of M'Carthy More were called "his *cane poble*,"[5] or people subject to his law and its penalties. Fines were various and numerous, and must have formed a

[1] *Campion*.   [2] Capt. B. Riche (of Colerane), p. 2.
[3] Present of Co. Waterford, 1537, Add. MS. 4819.
[4] S.P.O. 1550.   [5] Present of Cork, 1576, S.P.O.

considerable ingredient of income from a large and populous region.

The much reprobated practice of receiving *coigne* (made illegal on account of its abuse) was, besides being the original receipt of the chieftain, in fact his only means of subsistence when outside his territory, in times when the non-existence of either money or hostelries precluded him from aught but availing himself of the "old custom of giving meat and drinke."[1] There was an ancient usage in Galway of giving " *connome* and meales" to the leader of the Arran galloglasses and his men whenever they came to town.[2] Even in the metropolitan county, and in the 17th century, the receiving "*coigne* and livery" was partly the consideration for which land was let; it being stipulated in a lease dated 1613, that the lessee, the Archbishop of Dublin, should provide sufficient victual and lodging for two boys, with horse meat and stabling for three horses, on the premises, whenever the landlord, Sir R. Nugent, resorted to Dublin.[3]

Coigne or refection, when systematically due, was specially named the "custom of *cuddikie*," and warranted the chief in coming " with such company as pleaseth him to the lands charged with that tenure, and in taking meat and drink of the inhabitants thereof for the space of four meales, at four tymes of the yere."[4] This " custom " was, in fact, the quarterly rendering which appears by many antique records to have been the fundamental rent charge on land. When the *Ri* was on visits to his vassals under this usage, he was said "to have his people " or train " in *cosheric*"[5]— that is, taking his *cios* as a king. The provisions for the occasion seemed to have been obtained by assessment on the tribe holding the land, *cios* being a tribute or contribu-

[1] *Anno* 1535, S.P. II. 287.   [2] Hardiman's *Galway*, p. 207.
[3] *Pat.* 13 *Jac.* I. p. 280.   [4] Sir W. St. Leger.
[5] 1587, *Desmond's Rents*.

tion: hence is derived the word "cess," peculiar to Ireland, having the same root as the Latin and French terms that imply an assessment levied *tributim*, and anciently used to denote the charge upon the tenantry of "the Pale" of maintaining the troops of the crown. The method of collection by contribution was continued in the 17th century, for the purpose of supporting the needy descendants of dispossessed chieftains by "coshering." This practice was denounced by the Statute of 1634, because it sustained thousands of young "idel," or noble, swordsmen, who soon afterwards broke out into general insurrection to recover their lands; and who "cessed themselves, their followers, horses, and greyhounds upon the country," receiving "their *eaught* and *adraugh*, viz., supper and breakfast," and craving helps; to supply which, and their "entertainment," the country people made "cuts, levies, and plotments upon themselves."

Vassals who held land by the tenure of receiving their chieftain at *cuid-oidche* appear to have been of superior rank to the frank tenants of sorren-land, which was liable to "bonaght" for galloglasses.[1] The same custom prevailed, of course, in Gaelic Scotland. In the comparatively modern rent-roll of a Scots laird there occurs the—"*Item*, for *cuid-oidche*, 20s.," receivable yearly, if he did not use his right to lodge for one night in his tenant's house.[2] Curious as the practice is in its origin, it was subsequently well adapted to the requirements of a wide-spread clan, whose disputes with borderers often obliged their chieftain to visit the extremity of his territory. But it undoubtedly arose as a mode of maintenance; and, having become a "rent," was commuted in Ireland towards the close of the 16th century into a money payment. "Cuddihie," as rendered to the Earl of Clancarthy, is termed a "portion" to be spent either at the freeholder's house or sent to the earl's,

[1] 1587, *Desmond's Rents*.   [2] *Logan*, I. 212.

in a certain proportion of flesh, aqua vitae, ale, cows, and flour, or else in lieu, £4 8s. 8d. This composition had been effected by Government Commissioners, who valued this charge as due by certain monasteries, and *sorren* by others, at the same rate. Their labours (of which by-and-bye) seem to have been permanently successful in Munster. In the 17th century, O'Driscoll continued to pay M'Carthyreagh a sum equivalent to about £150 a year at present in lieu of entertaining him at supper;[1] and M'Brien Ara received some hard cash, with certain heads of various cattle, instead of all "customs, refections, impositions, or cess of horse and horse boys, contributions of sragh, sorohin, and bonnagh, duties, casualties, aids, benevolences or free gifts, cuttings, cosheries, or other advantages, claims, and demands."[2] But the tribes in the wilds of Connaught seem to have retained their old mode of rendering tribute; as appears by a record that a certain "clan" paid rent, as such, in the form of bread, drink, and flesh, at Christmas, and a proportion of bread, butter, and drink, at Easter, yearly."[3] When rent came into Lord Clancarthy in such gross and live forms as cattle, accompanied by loads of merchandise, to the pre-emption of which when landed at his seaports this chieftain was entitled, the arrival might have been announced to him like that of the bulky tribes the poet wrote of—

"Huge bales of British cloth block up your door,
A hundred oxen at your levee roar!"

[1] *Celtic Miscel.* 106.   [2] *Pat.* 6 *Jac.* p. 39.   [3] *W. Con.* 58.

NOTES.

1. p. 17—**Grassum**: a sum of money paid by the tenant to his landlord on entering into possession of his farm; or by the fiar to his superior on succeeding as heir.

2. p. 17—**Gule**: the corn marigold (*chrysanthemum segetum*). A farmer planting gule was to be punished as if he were a traitor leading a hostile army; and a serf so offending was to pay a fine of a sheep and to cleanse the land. [*Act Parlt.*, vol. i., pp. 750, 751.]

Lord Hailes says [*An. Scot.*, vol. ii., p. 339] that this statute was still enforced in his day in the barony of Tinwald in Annandale.

In the parish of Cargill in Perthshire a curious custom is recorded in the *Statistical Account*, vol. xiii., pp. 536, 537.

"An old custom takes place in this parish called *gool-riding*, which seems worthy of observation. The lands of Cargill were formerly so very much over-run by a weed with a yellow flower that grows among the corn, especially in wet seasons, called *gools*, and which had the most pernicious effects, not only upon the corns while growing, but also in preventing their *winning* when cut down, that it was found absolutely necessary to adopt some effectual method of extirpating it altogether. Accordingly, after allowing a reasonable time for procuring clean seed from other quarters, an Act of the Baron's Court was passed, enforcing an old Act of Parliament to the same effect, imposing a fine of 3s. 4d., or a wedder sheep, on the tenants, for every stock of *gool*, that should be found growing among their corns at a particular day, and certain persons stiled *gool-riders* were appointed to ride through the fields, search for *gool*, and carry the law into execution when they discovered it. Though the fine of a wedder sheep is now commuted and reduced to a 1d. sterling, the practice of *gool-riding* is still kept up and the fine rigidly exacted. The effects of this baronial regulation have been salutary, beyond what could have been expected. Five stocks of *gool* were formerly said to grow for every stock of corn through all the lands of the barony, and twenty throols of barley did not then produce one boll. Now the grounds are so cleared from this noxious weed, that the corns are in high request for seed; and after the most diligent search the *gool-riders* can hardly discover as many growing stocks of *gool* the fine for which will afford them a dinner and a drink."

3. p. 17—**Sauch**, or saugh : the common willow tree (*salix caprea*).

4. p. 18—**Ploughgate**: contains eight oxgangs of thirteen Scots acres each, or one hundred and four acres altogether. (See chapter on Weights and Measures.)

5. p. 20—**Beltane** : was the 1st of May old style.

6. p. 21—**Firlot** : the standard firlot was in the custody of the Burgh of Linlithgow. As a measure it varied very considerably. The alterations are given in full detail in the chapter on Weights and Measures.

7. p. 23—**Acta Dominorum Auditorum**, or the Acts of the Lord Auditors of Causes and Complaints, are given in the original records, along with the proceedings of the Three Estates in full Parliament; but those of the reigns of James III. and James IV., from 1466 to 1494, were published in a separate volume in 1839, containing much of the highest interest regarding the state of the country at that time as shown by the prices of commodities, the value of money, and other statistical information.

8. p. 23—**Boll** : see the chapter on Weights and Measures.

9. p. 23—**Merk** : was equal to thirteen shillings and fourpence Scots. The merk was only a money of account, but half-merks and quarter-merks were coined by James VI. in 1591, 1592, 1593, and a few in 1594. (See *Records of the Coinage of Scotland*, vol. i., p. clvii., pp. 118, 177, 253, and vol. ii., plate ix.)

10. p. 25—**To fee** : the term used in Scotland for hiring farm servants. Feeing fairs are not yet altogether extinct, at least in the west of Scotland.

11. p. 27—**Birleymen** : otherwise Burlie men, Burlaw men, or Byr-law men. This was an institution of high antiquity now almost unknown. Skene says :—" The laws of Burlaw ar maid and determined be consent of neichtbours elected and chosen be common consent in the courts called the Byrlaw courts in the quhilk cognition is taken of compaintes betuixt nichtbour and nichtbour. The quhilk men sa chosen as judges and arbitrators to the effect foresaid ar commonly called Byrlaw men."

In the *Reg. Maj.*, bk. iv., c. 39, c. 18, Birlaw courts are said to be ruled by the consent of neighbours. These existed in the north of Scotland so late as 1721. (See Jamieson's *Scot. Dict.*, *sub voce*.)

12. p. 27—**Thirled** : to *thirl* was to bind the tenants to grind their corn at some particular mill. Erskine defines *thirlage* as constituted by writing either directly or indirectly; and a proprietor could *thirl* his tenants by an act or regulation of his own court. (*Inst.*, bk. ii., tit. 9, s. 21.)

13. p. 27—**Multures.** The *multure* was the toll of the miller for grinding the grain into meal and was usually taken in kind. The ancient regulations about mills are very curious. By the assize of William I. if a man bought corn in one lordship to carry into another to grind, and stopped at a tavern to eat and drink, he had to pay the multure if he put the sacks in the house or on the midden; but he was free from the toll if he left the sacks in the king's highway. Burgesses of a burgh might use hand mills, but it was illegal for any others to do so. In 1640 all Sunday work was prohibited in mills.

14. p. 28—**Red Fish.** Regulations against killing unseasonable salmon, which were called red or black fish, are found at a very early period. The principal enactments are noticed in the chapter on the Fisheries.

15. p. 28—**Flyting.** Scolding or using bad language and quarrelling seems to have been a common imperfection amongst the women of Scotland in early times. The records of more modern police and petty session courts show that it is not altogether a relic of the past.

16. p. 35—**Rig** : that part of the web which is folded down or doubled.

17. p. 35—**Selvidge** : the rest of the web as distinguished from the rig.

18. p. 35—**Seal of cause.** A writ under the seal of the municipality conferring certain privileges on the particular craft. Thus the Cordiners of Glasgow had a seal of cause from the Lord Provost, Bailies, Council, and Community of the Burgh and City of Glasgow in 1558 in their favour which was confirmed under the seal of James, Archbishop of Glasgow.

In other cases the seal of cause was confirmed by Parliament.

19. p. 35—**Walker.** To "walk" or "wauk" cloth is to thicken it. Garnett in his tour in Scotland, gives an ingenious derivation of the term. He considers the operation as so-called because the women sit round a board and work the cloth with their feet as if walking. Wauk mills were in existence in Ayrshire and Renfrewshire till a very recent period.

20. p. 35—**Wobster**: a weaver. The word also occurs in the form of "webster" and "wabster."

21. p. 35—**Serplath**. A measure of wool equal according to Skene to eighty stones. (See chapter on Weights and Measures.)

22. p. 37. **Serges**: a sort of light cloth.

23. p. 37. **Growgrams**, otherwise grogranes or grograms: a kind of coarse silk taffety.

24. p. 37. **Bombesies**: a thin hard stuff.

25. p. 37. **Stemmingis**: a cloth originally made of goat's hair, afterwards of wool or silk. It is called also taminy.

26. p. 37. **Beyis**, or bayis: the cloth now called baize.

27. p. 38. **Schone**: shoes.

28. p. 39. **Sinderit**: parted or separated.

29. p. 40. **Plotter**: one who makes bare or smooth.

30. p. 40. **Camber**, or camester: a wool comber.

41. p. 40. **Scherar**: a wool dresser.

32. p. 40. **Spyner**: a wool spinner.

33. p. 42. **Kerseys**, or kairsays (see *Scots Acts*, vol. vi. 1. 727): a sort of cloth.

34. p. 44. **Seys**: a sort of coarse homespun cloth. (See Thom's *Hist. of Aberdeenshire*, ii. 151.)

35. p. 45. **Speir**: to search out; make diligent inquiry for.

36. p. 45. **Touk of Drume**: beat of drum.

37. p. 56. **Garnels**: granaries.

38. p. 60. **Lame**: earthernware.

39. p. 60. **Schryno**: a small casket or cabinet.

40. p. 64. **Doucat**, more commonly *dowcate*: a pigeon house. By an Act of James IV. in 1503, every laird was to have a park with deer, fish ponds, rabbit warrens and *dowcatis*.

42. p. 70. **Coups**, or *cowpis*: a sort of basket trap for catching fish at a fall.

42. p. 70. **Prins**, or *prynis*: another sort of fish trap.

43. p. 76. **Stallage**: money payable for the privilege of erecting a stall in the market.

NOTES. 187

44. p. 76. **Pined** : dried by exposure to the weather after salting.

45. p. 79. Since this was written an excellent index has appeared which entirely removes the complaint made.

46. p. 80. **Wageouris** : soldiers hired for pay.

47. p. 115. **Alderman** : an official of burghs in Scotland. This title, so well known south of the Tweed, was once a familiar one in Scotland. The "Assise Regis David" prohibited any alderman intromitting with the pleas of the crown. The "Leges Burgorum" ordered the alderman of each burgh to swear in twelve burgesses to maintain the laws. An Act of Parliament in 1425 enjoins the alderman and bailies of a burgh to hold wapenshaws four times a year. Provosts, aldermen, and bailies of burghs were ordered to fix the price of fish each market day by an Act of 1540. Shortly after this period the title fell into disuse.

48. p. 121. **Tome** : more frequently *tume* or *toom* : empty.

49. p. 128. **Pullici and Rembertini** : merchant companies of Italy who played an important part in the financial transactions of the Middle Ages. The Rembertini, like the Friscobaldi, Bardi, and Spini, had their head quarters in Florence. Others, as the Ballardi, belonged to Lucca.

50. p. 139. **Stented** : taxed or assessed.

INDEX.

Abbeys. See also *Monks*.
— Aberbrothock, 16 ; grants to, 92, 124.
— Cambuskenneth, grants to, 54, 107.
— Cupar, rental book of, 17.
— Dundrennan, grant to, 111.
— Glenluce, privilege of, 122.
— Holmcultram, privilege of, 112.
— Holyrood, 57 ; grants to, 54, 67, 71, 107.
— Kelso, 10, 16 ; grant to, 54.
— Melrose, grants to, 11, 13, 54, 108 ; 112.
— Scone, 16 ; grants to, 106, 110.
Aberbrothock, Abbot of. See *Abbeys*.
Aberdeen, Bishopric of, 22, 107 ; cloth factory in, 47 ; salmon exported from, 70, 71 ; rents customs, 87 ; its importance, 145, 147, 148 ; keeps standard measures, 152, 170.
Accounts of the Lord High Treasurer, 78.
Acta Sanctorum, 106.
Acts of the Parliaments of Scotland, 78.
Acta Dominorum Auditorum, 23.
Adraugh, 180.
Agriculture, different periods of, 1, 2 ; affected by difference in race, 2 ; at Roman invasion, 3 ; Romano-British or prehistoric period of, 3, 4, 5 ; amongst Dalriadic Scots, 4, 5 ; Celtic period of, 5 ; Early Feudal period, 9 ; promoted by monks, 10 ; laws relating to, 14, 19, 20, 23, 24 ; state of, 29.
Ailred of Rievaul, 4, 83, 107.
Airth, 54.
Alan of Galloway, 110.
Alderman, 115.
Ale, excise rates on, 99, 101, 102.
Alexander I., 106.
Alexander II., 14, 29, 92, 110.
Alexander III., 29, 34, 67, 84, 86, 92, 93, 121, 125, 126.

Alexander, Robert, 17.
Allan, Thomas, 45.
Alum, 120.
Amargin Mac Ecelsalech, 32.
Amra-Choluim-Chilli, 7.
Amsterdam, trade with, 149.
Antwerp, trade with, 131, 132, 137, 143.
Aqua Vitae, excise rates on, 99, 102.
Arbroath. See Aberbrothock.
Archæological Association, Ayr and Galloway, 26.
Archæological Mis., 175.
Archæological Tracts, II., 173.
Ardbracan, 175.
Argyll, Bishop of, 81 ; county of and taxation, 102.
Armour, James, 45.
Army, cloth for, 47.
Arran, 7.
Artillery, small, 95.
Assisa de Ponderibus, 163.
Assisa de Tolloneis, 48, 60, 119.
Assize of Aberdeen, 170.
Assize of Measures and Weights, David I., 152, 157, 159.
Assize of Weights and Measures, James I., 160, 164.
Assisa Regis David, 161.
Assise Willelmi Regis, 108.
Athole, Duke of, 57.
Avenel, Robert, 11.
Ayr, foreign weavers in, 40 ; cloth factory in, 45 ; saltpans near, 54 ; a port, 71, 113, 150; its importance, 145, 147 ; had peculiar measures, 155 ; county of, tax on, 97.
Baert, George, 40.
Bailie, 27.
Bailies, restrictions on, 119 ; duties of, 152.
Bain, Joseph, 109, 111.
Balgarvie, 16.

Ballivi ad extra, 84.
Banff, its salmon export, 71.
Banko, John, 36.
Barbur, John, 18.
Barley, early mention of, 4, 12 ; prices of, 15, 23 ; import of, 136 ; corns of, standard of measure, 158.
Barons, rights of, 119.
Baron Officer, 27.
Battry, 120.
Beans, prices of, 12, 16 ; regulations regarding cultivation of, 19, 21, 25 ; article of trade, 120 ; how measured, 165.
Bear. See *Bere*.
Beer, excise rates on, 99, 101, 102, 136 ; how measured, 165, 166.
Bell, James, 45.
Bellie, 26.
Bells, casting of, 64.
Beltane, 20.
Bere, price of, 23, 25 ; rent part paid in, 26 ; measure of, 165, 166.
Berwick, saltpans near, 56 ; its salmon export, 71 ; its importance, 108, 114 ; its merchant guild, 113 ; port dues, 121 ; privileges, 124.
Bewlie, 70.
Beyis, 37.
Bickit, John, 28.
Birley-men, 11, 20, 27.
Bischop, Gabriel, 40.
Blackeland, 54.
Blair, Giles, 23.
Bleaching, 48, 49, 51.
Boats, fishing, cost of, 72, 73.
Bolden, Barony of, 11.
Bombesies, 37.
Bonaght, 174, 176, 180.
Bonnington, cloth factory in, 45 ; bleaching fields at, 51.
Bo'ness, 147.
Book of Kells, 33.
Book of Rights, 32.
Borders, taxes for defence of, 95.
Bottles, manufacture of, 58, 59.
Bowers, 26.
Bowers, Steel, 26.
Brandy, 64.
Brazil, 120.
Bread, wheaten, 13.
Brehon Laws, 32.
Brehon, The, 7.
Brew-houses, 12, 119.
Bridges, taxes for, 96.
Broch, of Dunbeath, 4.
Bruce, Robert, 88, 93, 127, 129, 151, 152.
Bryson, Margaret, 28.

Buannacht bona, 176.
Buchan, Alexander, Earl of, 124.
Burgh Laws, 157.
Burghs, Royal, privileges of, 30, 34, 39, 41, 50, 75, 83, 109, 143 ; establishment of, 82 ; rents of, a source of revenue, 84, 87 ; weights and measures in, 154.
Burial laws, 50.
Burleigh, Lady, 55.
Burnett, Mr., 136.
Burntisland, its importance, 145, 147.
Bushes, 68.
Butchers, regulations concerning, 25, 117, 119.
Bute, 7 ; taxation in, 102.
Butter, prices of, 23 ; trade in, 120, 148, 160 ; as rent in Ireland, 174, 175, 177.
Buttons, 32.
Cæsar, Julius, 3.
Cains, 178. See also *Can*.
Caithness, Earl of, 86.
Caldrons, 120.
Calentyr, 54.
Calpe, 82.
Cambuskenneth. See *Abbeys*.
Camber, 40.
Camden, 177.
Campbell, Daniel, 63, 64.
Campbell, George, 57.
Campbell, John, 150.
Campbell, Matthew, 63, 64.
Campvere, trade with, 133, 142 ; Scotch church in, 144.
Can, 8, 81.
Can-finny, 173, 175.
Candles, part rent, 9.
Candlewicks, 62.
Cannons, casting of, 64.
Canongate, 42.
Canvas, 120.
Carew MS., 175, 177.
Carles, 10.
Capons, 22.
Carrick, 8.
Cartwright, John, 146.
Cassius, Dion, 3.
Castle wards, payments of, a source of revenue, 84, 87.
Cattle, 13 ; used for ploughing, 14 ; prices of, 15, 16, 23 ; export of, 25, 89, 135 ; *Conveth* paid in, 9, 81 ; fines paid in, 86 ; rent paid in, 88, 173 ; taxes on, 95, 99, 120.
Cawpe, 82.
Celtic Miscellanies, 181.
Celtic Society, 32.

INDEX.   191

Celts, 6, 8, 9; industries among, 31, 32, 33.
Census, 86.
Cess, 180.
Chamberlain, Scottish, 83, 87; duties of, 152.
Chariots, making of, 65.
Charles I., 42, 72.
Charles II., 99.
Charters, of Arbroath, 7.
— of Bolden, 11.
— of Durham, 106.
— of Edinburgh, 130, 131.
— of Glasgow, 34, 119.
— of Melrose, 13.
— of Moray, 7.
— of Scone, 7, 9, 6, 16, 81, 92.
— of feu farm, 87.
Chartularies. See *Charters.*
Cheese, 13, 120; rent, part paid in, 9, 22, 85; price of, 23; how weighed, 160.
Cheueronys, 120.
Chieftains, Irish, their rent, 173, 174, 175, 176, 177, 178; customs regarding, 177, 178, 179.
Cillé Choca, 32.
Cinel Angus, 7, 8.
Cinel Eoghain, 178.
Cinel Gabran, 7.
Cinel Lorn, 7, 8.
Cios, 179.
Ciphi. See *Cups.*
Circuit Courts, 86.
Civil Service, beginnings of, 80.
Claers, James, 40.
Clancarthy, Earl of, 180, 181.
Clasps, 32.
Claverhouse, John Graham of, 46.
Cloaks, of wool, 32; mottled, 32.
Cloth (see also *Manufactures, woollen*), bordered, 31; of gold, 32; dyeing of, 31, 32, 34; measuring of, 35, 155; trade in, 135; duties on, 136.
Coaches, making of, 65.
Coach-harness, making of, 65.
Coal, trade in, 147, 148, 149.
Coal fish. See *Colemoth.*
Coca, 32.
Cockburn, Captain Ninian, 139.
Cod, 89, 120.
Coigne, 174, 175, 176, 179.
Coigne and livery, 179.
Coigne-bon, 174.
Coinage, 82; a source of revenue, 84, 91; made free, 91; revenue from, at Union, 103.
Coinmedha. See *Conveth.*

Coinme, 175, 176.
Colemoth, 120.
Comeric, 178.
Commissioners of Royal Burghs, 39, 40, 41, 139, 140, 142.
Commission, Royal Executive, for encouragement of Scottish industries, 42; powers of, 43.
Compositions, 84, 87.
Commonwealth, taxes during, 97, 98; proceeds of Excise before, 101.
Conchobar, Mac Nessa, 31.
Conies, 17.
Connome and meales, 179.
Conon, 70.
Conservator, 131, 132, 137, 140, 141, 143; Court of, 131.
Convention of Royal Burghs, ordinances of, relating to cloth manufacture, 35, 39, 40, 41, 42; to export of wool, 37, 38; to linen manufacture, 50, to letters of marque, 135; to foreign trade, 137, 138, 141, 142, 143; to condition of towns, 149; to weights and measures, 151, 153, 154, 155, 156.
Convention of Royal Burghs, *Records of,* 136, 142, 144.
Conveth, 8, 9, 60, 81. See also *Cuddicke.*
Conyan. See *Cuddicke.*
Coquet, 141.
Cordwan, 120.
Corn (see also *Barley, Oats, Rye,* and *Wheat*), cultivation of, 4, 5, 21; Indian, 25; export of, 25; as part rent, 85, 177; trade in, 111, 112, 113, 120, 122, 136.
Corse, John, 5, 63.
Corshill, Barony of, 27; Court book of, 26; Court of, 27, 28.
Corstorphine, bleaching fields at, 51.
Cosherie, 175, 176, 178, 179, 180.
Costage, 94.
Cottarii. See *Cottars.*
Cottars, 10, 17, 18, 26.
Council of Trade, 75.
Coups, 70.
Crail, 71, 145.
Crannogs, 4.
Creaght, 173.
Cro, 86, 173.
Crochat, John, 19.
Crofters, 22, 26.
Cromwell, Oliver, 44, 100, 101.
Crops, cereal, 5, 12; protection of, 13, 24; rotation of, 17, 19, 20; state of, 29.

Crown, support of, 81 ; grants to, 92, 93, 94, 96, 99.
Crown lands, 84, 85, 93 ; rents, value of at Union, 103.
Crown vassals, casualties of, source of revenue, 84, 86.
Crusaders, 121.
Cuddicke. See *Conveth* and *Custom of Cuddikie*.
Cuid, 175.
Cuid oidche, 175, 176, 180.
Culross, 145.
Culverings, 95.
Cumin seed, 120.
Cuningar, 19.
Cunningham, 8.
Cunninghame, Robert, 56.
Cunningham, Sir David, 29.
Cupar. See *Abbeys*.
Cups, 136.
Cure Masters of Fish, 132.
Currency, national, 80, 82.
Custom of Cuddikie, 81, 82, 179.
Customs (see also *Taxes* and *Revenue*), on cloth, 35, 89 ; on linen, 48, 49 ; on salt, 56, 90 ; on glass, 58 ; on soap, 60 ; on fish, 70, 89 ; returns from, 72, 88, 89, 90 ; on skins, 88, 89 ; on horses, sheep, and cattle, 89 ; exemptions from, 43, 107 ; great customs, 84, 88, 89 ; annexed to Crown, 90 ; increase of, 95 ; value of, at Union, 103 ; negotiations concerning, 137, 143.
Custumars, 84, 88 ; powers of, 98.
Dairies, 13.
Dairsie, Laird of, 37.
Dalriadic Scots, 4, 5, 33 ; tribes among, 7.
Dalyell, General, 46.
Damages, 12, 15.
David I., 8, 34, 51, 54, 67, 71, 72, 73, 74, 75, 76, 80, 82, 83, 85, 88, 106, 107, 152, 157, 162.
David II., 88, 91, 92, 94, 129.
Davyes, Sir John, 174.
Dawick, Laird of, 145.
Deacons, collectors of Excise, 100.
Debtors, 24.
Dee, 69.
Defence, national, 80, 82.
Demesne, 85.
Dempster, 27.
Dermis, Cornelius, 40.
Desmond, Earl of, 174, 175.
Deveron, 70.
Dick, Sir William, 100.

Dickson, Robert, 52.
Dog, Walter, 19.
Don, 69.
Doucats, 64.
Douglas, Robert, 59, 61.
Draining, 17, 18.
Dress, among Celtic tribes, 31, 32 ; laws against wearing silk, 51 ; regulations concerning, 137.
Druggets, 49.
Dryhouse Cottars, 26.
Dumbarton, a fishing port, 71, 72 ; its standard measures, 155.
Dumfries, 154.
Duncan of Carrick, 54.
Dundee, foreign weavers in, 40 ; salmon exported from, 70, 71 ; its importance, 145, 147, 148 ; its shipping, 149.
Dundrennan. See *Abbeys*.
Dunfermline. See *Monks*.
Dunwich, Scotch community at, 122, 123.
Dupin, Nicholas, 62, 63.
Durham, Cathedral of, 106.
Eaught, 176, 180.
Edgar, 106.
Edinburgh, foreign websters in, 37, 39, 42 ; export of wool from, 37 ; rents petty customs, 87 ; tax on town and county, 97 ; its importance, 145 ; its shipping, 149 ; keeps standard measures, 152, 157, 159, 170.
Edward I., 127.
Edward II., 128.
Edward III., 134.
Eggs, part rent paid in, 9.
Elcho, Lord, 59.
Elders, collectors of Excise, 100.
Elgin, salmon exported from, 70, 71.
Ellbed. See *Elnwand*.
Elnwand, 159.
Embassies, expenses of, 95.
Embroidery, 32.
Erskine, William, 57.
Escheats, 84.
Ewin, Sir, of Erregeithill, 81.
Exchequer, 86.
Excise, first notice of, 99 ; duties levied, 99, 100, 101, 102 ; collectors of, 100 ; farming of, 100, 101 ; proceeds of, 101, 102, 103 ; difficulties in collecting, 102 ; exemptions from, 51, 131.
Exemptions, from taxes or customs, 37, 41, 43, 44, 45, 46, 47, 49, 51, 52, 76, 88, 92 ; from military service,

44, 45; from billeting of soldiers, 51.
Expedition and hosting, 9, 82.
Export, of corn, 25.
— of cattle, 25, 89, 135.
— of malt, 38.
— of schone, 38.
— of linen, 38, 49.
— of salt, 38, 55.
— of glass, 58.
— of salmon, 70, 71, 135.
— of fish, 71, 89, 120, 148.
— of wool and woollen goods, 35, 36, 37, 38, 41, 42, 66, 88, 89, 111, 135, 148.
— of hides, 88, 135, 149.
— of horses, sheep, 89, 135.
— of coal, 147, 148.
— of wine, 135.
— of tallow, 135.
Extent. See *Valuation Roll*.
Extentors, 95.
Factories, Cloth, establishment of, in Edinburgh, 36, 37, 40, 45, 47; and burghs, 41, 42; in Haddington, 44; in Glasgow, 45, 46, 47; spread of, 45, 47: Glass, 57, 58, 59; Linen, 50, 51; Silk, 52.
Falaise, Treaty of, 92.
Famines, 15, 24.
Farthingmen, 115.
Feacht, 8, 9, 81, 82.
Feilire Aenghuis, 32.
Fermant, Philip, 36.
Ferme, 25, 26.
Feu-duty, 86.
Figs, 120.
Fields, enclosed, 11.
File, The, 7.
Findruine, 32.
Findthorn, 69.
Fingram, 49.
Fines (see also *Penalties*), agricultural, 13, 14, 18, 20, 21, 24, 25; for contumacy of Baron Court, 27; criminal, 27, 28, 29, 86, 178; for infringing trade rights, 34, 58; for exporting wool, 38; for using woollen grave clothes, 50; for infringement of *Statuta Gilde*, 116, 117, 118, 119; a source of revenue, 84, 87, 178; religious, 144; on burghs for not providing weights, 154.
Fischer, Thomas, 40.
Fisheries, 67: Fishery Company, 72; limits of, 74; privileges of, 75: Fishing trade, 107, 111, 120, 132,

148; privileges of, 76: Salmon, salting of, 55; rights, 67; laws, 67; close time, 68; importance of, 69; export of, 70, 71, 135. 171; customs, 70, 71, 89, 130; price of, 70; rivers, 69; revenue from, 90: Trout, laws concerning, 70: Pike, laws concerning, 70: Herring, laws concerning, 71, 75, 76; duty on, 71, 89, 90; packing of, 76; revenue from, 72, 90; measure of barrels, 72, 76, 90, 171; export of, 120, 148: White fish, duty on, 80, 90.
Flaths, 6.
Fleming, James, 38.
Fletcher, George, 75.
Fordun, 15.
Forester, Sir John, 162.
Forfar, 81.
Foulis, Thomas, 41.
Four-Masters, 176.
Fowler. See *Game*.
Fuan. See *Tunic*.
Fustians, 37.
Gael, The, Logan, 177, 180.
Galloway, 8, 9, 12.
Gairm-sluaigh, 174.
Game, 19, 22.
Gardin, John, 36.
Garnels, 56.
Ginger, 120.
Giraldus Cambrensis, 178.
Glammis, 81.
Glasgow, Burgh of, privileges, 34; cloth factories in, 45, 46, 47; glass work in, 59; sugar works, 63; tax on, 97; its importance, 145, 147; foreign trade, 148.
Glasgow, Chartulary of, 34, 119.
Glasgow, Church of, 8.
Glass, works, 57, 58, 59; window, 58; price of, 58; tax on, 58; export and import of, 58; mirror, 58; coach, moulded, 59; privileges of trade, 58, 59; polished, 59.
Glebe, measure of, 169.
Glenluce. See *Abbeys*.
Gordon, James, 64.
Gordon estates, 25.
Grange, 10.
Grass maill, 27.
Grassum, 17, 22.
Growgrams, 37.
Guicciardini, Lodovico, 133, 134.
Guilds, merchant, 109; Berwick, its fines and penalties, 115-119; its

benefits, 116; its privileges, 117; its government, 118.
Gule, 14, 17.
Gunpowder, acts concerning, 64, 65; import of, 64, 65; factories, 65.
Haco, 125.
Haddington, a seat of woollen manufacture, 44.
Haddock, 120.
Hagbuts, 95.
Halkett, George, 141, 143.
Halyburton, Ledger of, 144.
Hamburg, trade with, 149; measure of, 170.
Hamilton, Frederick, 63.
Hamilton, James, 45.
Hamilton, John, 63.
Harbiestone, George, 28.
Hardiman's Galway, 179.
Harper, Janet, 28.
Harris Ware, 176.
Hart's-head, 13.
Harvest-work, 4.
Hats, manufacture of, 66; import of, 66; duty on, 100.
Hay, Sir George, 57, 58.
Hay, John, 75.
Hay of Leys, 16.
Health, public, 116.
Heare, Peter Groot, 61.
Hemp, 65.
Henre de Turk, 40.
Henry III., 100, 125, 130.
Herbs, garden, 4.
Heriot, 173.
Herring. See *Fisheries*.
Hides, export of, 88; revenue from, 90; trade in, 117, 126, 135, 149; duties on, 88, 136.
Holmcultram. See *Abbeys*.
Holyrood. See *Abbeys*.
Honey, 121.
Hoops, 148.
Hope, Sir Alexander, 65.
Horses, 14, 120; prices of, 13, 15, 23; duty on, 89, 121; export of, 89, 135.
Hospital, 116.
Hunter, Andrew, 40, 41.
Husbandmen, 10, 18.
Husbandi. See *Husbandmen*.
Husbandland, 10.
Ich, 81, 82.
Idlers, 43, 49.
Import of cloth, 35, 46.
— of timber, 38, 120, 149.
— of wool, 43.
— of linen, 48, 49, 105.
— of silk, 51.

Import of salt, 55, 112, 136, 149, 155.
— of soap, 60, 136.
— of glass, 58.
— of gunpowder, 65.
— of hats, 66.
— of luxuries, 106.
— of corn, 110, 112, 122, 148.
— of meal, 110, 148.
— of wine, 111, 112, 120, 136, 150.
— of provisions, 120, 128, 136, 148, 149, 136, 150, 155.
— of dyes, 120.
— of spices, 120.
— of kitchen utensils, 120.
— of drugs, 120.
— of leather, 120.
— of oil, 120.
— of armour and weapons, 128, 135.
— of wooden goods, 148.
— of rosin, 149.
— of tar, 150.
— of iron, 150.
— Act against, 47.
Impost (under *Taxes*), Irish, on land, 173.
Inchgarde, 135.
Industries, 54. See also *Casting, Coach-building, Glass, Gunpowder, Iron, Oil, Paper, Porcelain, Pottery, Salt, Soap, Sugar.*
In field, 20.
Innerwich, 16.
Innes, Cosmo, 25, 133, 144.
Insula regis, 67.
Inverness, 147.
Ioch. See *Ich*.
Iron, 57, 120, 150; weights for, 160.
Irvine, revenue from herring, 72; its importance, 146; its standard measures, 155.
Isla, 7.
Jacque de la Rudge, 40.
James, The, 149.
James I., 70, 89, 94, 152, 157, 160.
James III., 90.
James VI., 30, 36, 41, 42.
James VII., 99, 158.
Janson, Arane, 40.
Jedburgh. See *Monks*.
Joceline, 5.
John, 124.
John, Duke of Brabant, 128.
Johnstone, John, 45.
Jousy, Robert, 41.
Jug, Stirling Pint, 162; description of, 163.
Jura, 7.
Justiciars, 84, 86.

Justice, administration of, 80, 86.
Kail, 17.
Kelso. See *Abbeys*.
Kelyng, 120.
Kempery men, 173.
Kenkonal, 8.
Kerseys, 42.
Kid, 22.
Kilcock. See *Cillé Choca*.
Kilwinning. See *Monks*.
Kintyre, 7.
Kirk, Trinity, 37.
Kirkcudbright, 145, 154.
Knives, 120.
Kyle, 8.
Kyncarrekyn, 67.
Kyncrech, 19.
Lame, 60.
L'Amey, Hugo, 69.
Lanark, keeps standard measures, 157; stone weight of, 161; county of, tax on, 97.
Lanark, Earl of, 145.
Land (see also *Tenure, Lease*), laws relating to, 14; divisions of, 20; holdings, 25; taxes on, 93; revenue from, 103; Tribe land, 6; Crown lands, 16, 21; Church lands, 21.
Law, merchants', 131.
Lawsuits, 28, 109, 122, 123.
Lead, 149.
Leases, 16, 17; conditions attached to, 17; forfeiture of, 20; Acts of Parliament concerning, 21; length of, 26.
Leblanc, 59.
Legal Antiquities, 25.
Leges Burgorum, 34, 82.
Leith, linen factory in, 51; glass work at, 58, 59; soap work at, 60, 61; sugar work in, 63; a fishing port, 71; its importance, 147.
Lepers, 18, 68, 116.
Leslie, Colonel Ludovic, 56.
Letters of gift, 84, 87.
Leven, Loch, 70.
Lews, The, 73.
Lex Mercatoria, 130.
Life of S. Columba, 105.
Life of S. Kentigern, 107.
Linen. See *Manufactures*.
Ling, 120.
Linlithgow, Earl of, 65.
Linlithgow, has standard measures, 154, 157, 167.
Linn, George, 60.
Lint, 12, 65.
Litster, 36.

Loans, 96.
Lockhart, George, 149.
Locks, 120.
London, the liberties of, 124.
Losseir, Claus, 40.
Lucas the Scot, 122.
Luscy, G. de, 109.
Lyell, James, 65.
Macbeth, 105.
M'Brien Ara, 181.
M'Carthy More, 174, 178.
M'Carthyreagh, 181.
M'Lean, Laughlan, 9.
Magistrates, powers of, 54, 84.
Magnus of Norway, 125.
Mains, 10.
Makers, 56.
Malars. See *Husbandi*, 10.
Malcolm III., 106.
Malcolm IV., 9, 3, 81, 92.
Malt, prices of, 12, 16; part rent, 22, 85; export of, 38; duty on, 102; trade in, 120, 136.
Malynes, Gerard, 129.
Manes, Denis, 63.
Manufactures, linen, 48-51.
— — earliest mention of, 48.
— — import and export of, 38, 49, 105.
— — enactments concerning, 48, 49, 50, 51.
— — breadth and measuring of, 49, 51.
— — custom duties, 48, 49.
— — prices of, 49.
— — bleaching of, 49, 51.
— — privileges of, 49, 51.
— — sealing of, 51.
— — wearing of, 51.
Manufactures, silk, 51-53; early mention of, 51; wearing of, 51; privileges of, 52; enactments concerning, 52.
Manufactures, woollen, 30-47. See also *Cloth*.
— — monopolies of royal burghs in, 30.
— — oldest existing specimen of, 33.
— — enactments concerning, 32, 34, 35, 36, 37, 38, 39, 40, 41, 42, 43, 45, 46, 47.
— — export and import of, 35, 42, 43, 46, 89; prohibitions against, 35, 36, 38, 41, 47.
— — duties on, 35, 89.
— — sealing of, 35, 36.
— — Flemish and Dutch weavers of, 36, 37, 39, 40, 42.
— — schools for teaching, 44.
— — privileges of, 37, 38, 41, 43, 44, 45, 46, 47.

Manufactures, woollen, seats of, 44, 45, 46.
— — Incorporations, 35, 46.
— — linen manufacture and, 51.
— — revenue from, 90.
Manure, 17, 25.
Marianus Scotus, 106.
Mark, its amount, 88.
Mart, rent paid in, 22, 25, 177.
Mart-land, 177.
Marsh-land, 17.
Melrose. See *Monks*.
Mary, Queen, 138, 139.
Masters, 56.
Masters and Men, customs in salt trade, 56.
Maule, Patrick, 61.
Maunsel, Samuel, 130.
Meal, 12; prices of, 15, 23; as part rent, 9, 22, 25, 174, 175; import of, 148; how measured, 165, 166.
Measures, 151; standard, 152, 156, 157, 164, 165, 166, 170; for foreign goods, 155; for native goods, 155; ancient standards, 163; Tables of measurement, 167, 168; heaped, 164; straik, 153, 164; victual, 164; water, 153.
— Boll, 23, 155, 163; standard, 167; bow, 167; bushel, 167; chalder, 167; choppin, 155, 163; fiddes, 161; firlot, 21, 152, 156, 164, 166; forpit, 167; gallon, Scots, 161; imperial, 163; gill, 164; half-firlot, 152, 164; jowcat, 164; last, 161; lippies, 167; mett, 153, 171; mutchkin, 155, 163; peck, 152, 154, 164, 167; pint, 152, 155, Stirling, 163; English, 166; quart, 155; sack, 161; stoup, 155.
— Land; acre, 168, standard, 166; davach, 169; ell, standard, 169; fall, 168; lineal and square, 169; mark-land, 169; ounce-land, 169; oxgang, 169; penny-land, 169, 170; plank, 170; plough-land, 169; rood, of baronies, 168, of burghs, 168, standard, 169, of mason's work, 196.
— Lineal: ell, 153, 155; foot, 158; inch, 157; mile, 158; yard, 158.
— Fishing; barrels, 170, marking of, 170; salmon, 170, 171; herrings, 170; west country, 170; hogshead, 170.
Meikle, John, 64.
Melrose. See *Abbeys*.
Melville, Earl of, 50.

Menteith, Walter, Earl of, 124.
Mercery, 120.
Merchants, liberties of, 109; foreign, 109, 129; religious restrictions on, 143, 144.
Merk, 2, 23.
Middleburgh, 129, 132, 133.
Mills, wind and water, 13; Dalry, 61, 62.
Mint, The, 91.
Minutes of Parliament, 43.
Money, 8, 11.
Monk, General, 98.
Monks. See also *Abbeys*.
— Cistertian, grant to, 92.
— of Dunfermline, grant to, 107.
— of Jedburgh, grants to, 54.
— of Kilwinning, grant to, 112.
— of Newbattle, grant to, 54.
— of Vauday, grant to, 111.
Monopolies, abolition of, 65.
Montgomerie, Hugh, 63.
Montgomerie, James, 59, 61, 63.
Montgomery, William, 60.
Montrose, salmon export, 71; its importance, 145; shipping of, 148.
Morrison's Haven, glass-work, 59.
Morton, Earl of, 75.
Mulones, 89.
Multures, 27.
Murder, fine for, 86.
Museum, National, of Antiquities, 33.
Musselburgh, cloth factory in, 47.
Nativi, 85.
National Assembly, 92.
Neil of Carrick, 8.
Neill, John, 45.
Nesbit, Henry, 140, 141.
Ness, 70.
Nets, fishing, cost of, 70; trade in, 120.
Newbattle. See *Monks*.
New Mills, 45, 46; Company, 47.
Newmilns, 62.
New Sugar Manufactory of Glasgow, 63.
Nicoll, 101.
Nith, 70.
Nugent, Sir R., 179.
Nungate, 44.
Oats, part rent, 9, 22; prices of, 12, 15, 23; taxes on, 95; trade in, 148; how measured, 165, 166.
Oatmeal. See *Meal*.
O'Callaghan, 175.
O'Conor, 177, 178.
O'Curry, Eugene, 32.
O'Donoughue, 175.
O'Donovan, Dr., 5.

O'Doyne, 178.
O'Driscoll, 181.
O'Neill, 176, 177.
O'Reilly, Sir John, 177.
Oil, making of, 65, 66 ; trade in, 120, 121.
Oliphant, of Gask, 68.
Ophaly, 177.
Orkney, land measures ir., 169, 170.
Ormeston, silk manufacturer, 52.
Out field, 20.
Owners and occupiers, 6, 8, 16, 22.
Oxgate, 10.
Oysters, 120.
Pac. Heb. I., 177.
Paper, works, 61, 62, 63 ; foreign workmen, 62 ; writing, 62 ; water mark, 62 ; privileges of trade, 63.
Parliament, Irish, Acts of, 175, 176, 180.
Parliament, Scottish, Acts of, for encouraging agriculture, 19, 20, 21, 23, 24, 25 ; for encouraging manufactures, 30, 35, 36, 39, 41, 42, 45, 46, 47, 48, 49, 50, 51, 55, 58, 59, 60, 61, 62, 63, 64, 65 ; for regulating fisheries, 67, 68, 70, 71, 72, 74, 75, 76 ; grants to the Crown, 99 ; customs, 102 ; for encouraging foreign trade, 129, 134, 145 ; for regulating weights and measures, 152, 153, 154, 158, 159, 160, 162, 171.
Paris, Matthew, 12.
Parva custuma, 87.
Pasturage, 13, 14, 20 ; irrigation of, 17.
Patrick of Dunbar, 13.
Pat. Jac. I., 173, 179, 181.
Pearls, Scotch, 106.
Pease, 12, 19, 21, 25, 120 ; prices of, 23 ; how measured, 165.
Peats, 17.
Penalties (see also *Fines*), for injury to crops, cattle, and ploughs, 24 ; for making inferior cloth, 35 ; for bleaching with lime, 49 ; infringing fishing laws, 68, 70 ; for failure in branding fish barrels, 170.
Pendiclers, 26.
Pennies, silver, 80, 87, 91.
Pepper, 120, 149.
Perth, foreign weavers in, 40 ; silk factory in, 52 ; salmon exported from, 70, 71 ; its importance, 145 ; has standard measures, 152.
Petersen, Jacob, 40.
Picken, Hugh, 29.
Picts, Northern, 7.

Pike. See *Fisheries*.
Pined, 76.
Pitchersgill, Simon, 45.
Plaiding, export of, 148.
Planting, 17, 23.
Plotter, 40 n.
Plough-gate, 8, 11, 18, 25 ; rent of, 22.
Plough-land, 169 ; rent on, 177.
Ploughing, 4 ; use of oxen in, 5, 14, 21, 22.
Porcelaine, 60.
Post Office, value of revenue from, at Union, 103.
Pottery, 57, 120 ; acts in favour of, 60 ; monopoly in, 60.
Poultry, part rent, 9, 22, 25, 85.
Present of Cork, 178.
Present of Co. Waterford, 178.
Prices, of cereals, 12, 15, 23 ; of malt, 12 ; of horses, 13, 15, 23 ; of sheep, 15, 23 ; of meal, 15, 23 ; of oxen and cows, 15, 16, 23 ; of pigs, 15 ; of butter, 23 ; of cheese, 23 ; of wool, 23 ; of linen, 49 ; of salt, 54 ; of glass, 58 ; of soap, 60 ; of salmon, 70 ; of herring, 73 ; of ling and cod, 73 ; of boats and fittings, 72, 122.
Primside, 14.
Prins, 70.
Privileges (see also *Exemptions*), merchants', 131, 132, 133, 143.
Privy Council, Scotland, and cloth manufature, 38, 39, 40, 41, 43 ; and foreign weavers, 42 ; and linen manufacture, 50 ; and silk manufacture, 52 ; monopolies and licenses granted by, 58, 59, 60, 61, 62 ; prohibitions of, 62 ; and fisheries, 72, 73 ; and measurements, 165, 171.
Proceedings of the Society of Antiquaries in Scotland, 169.
Prunes, 149.
Public Record Office, 109, 126.
Public officer, Irish, 177.
Pullici, 128.
Purslane. See *Porcelaine*.
Querns, 4, 13.
Quirren pottle, 174.
Rags, 62.
Raisins, 120.
Rape seeds, 65.
Rath, 7.
Ray, Gilbert, 19.
Record Edition of Acts of Parliament, 41.
Records of the Convention of Royal Burghs, 136, 142, 144.

Reddendo, 86, 87.
Reek-hen, 12, 25.
Register House, 17, 78.
Register of All Hallows, 176.
Register of the Convention of Royal Burghs, 78, 79.
Register of the Great Seal, 78.
Register of the Privy Council, 78.
Rembertini, 128.
Renfrew, county of, tax on, 97.
Rent, part paid in service, 8, 9, 10, 11, 16, 17, 22; of cottars, 10, 12; of husbandi, 11; of mill, 12; of brewhouses, 12; of lands, 16, 17; of house and land, 18; security for, 18; of a plough-gate, 22, 25; of woollen factory, 46; of land in burghs, 85, 87; taxes on, 95; Irish, in cattle, 173, 177; in victual, 173, 174, 175, 177, 179, 180, 181; in money, 175, 180, 181; in drink, 176, 181.
Revenue, 77; earliest provisions for regular, 82; officers, 83, 84; collectors of, 84, 87; sources of, 84; how paid, 80, 81, 82, 85; amounts of, 72, 87, 88, 89, 90, 136; increase of customs, 95; supplies, 99; excise, 99; sources of, at Union, 103.
Ri, maintenance of, 175, 178, 179.
Ribbons, tax on, 46.
Rice, 120.
Richard I., grants paid to, 92, 108.
Riche, Captain B., 178.
Rig, 6, 35.
Roads, 13.
Robert II., 136.
Robert, Count of Flanders, 127, 128.
Robert de Bernhame, 114.
Roche, Eustachius, 55.
Roger de Scalebroc, 54.
Roland of Carrick, 8.
Roland of Galloway, 13, 54.
Rolls of the Exchequer, 78, 81, 85, 91, 136.
Rooks, 20, 21.
Rosin, imported, 149.
Roxburgh, Earl of, 75.
Ruffus, John, 111, 112.
Ruffus, Richard, 113.
Rye, 12, 19; prices of, 13; taxes on, 95; how measured, 165.
Saggart, The, 7.
Sailors, regulations regarding, 143.
Salaries, for overseer of cloth factory, 45.
Salmon (see *Fisheries*).
Salt, export of, 38; making of, 54;

excise duties on, 102; trade in, 112, 120, 136, 147, 148, 149; measure of, 155, 165; used as a symbol, 177.
Saltcoats, 56.
Satellitum potare, 176.
Saxons, in Scotland, 33.
Scone, Abbey of, 16, 60, 67.
Scherar, 40.
Schone, export of, 38.
Schryno, 60.
School fees, 28.
Schools, technical, first, 44, 46.
Scone. See *Abbeys*.
Scot. Dic., 19.
Scott, Colonel James, 56.
Scott, William, 65.
Scot's White Paper Manufactory, 63.
Seaforth, Earl of, 73.
Seals, of cause, 35; cloth, 35, 37; linen, 51.
Sedans, making of, 65.
Seigniorage, 91.
Selvidge, 35.
Serges, 37, 49.
Serplath, 35.
Servants, farm, 24, 25.
Service, military, Scottish, 9, 24, 80, 82; exemptions from, 44, 45.
—— Irish, 173, 174, 175, 176, 180.
Setwell, 120.
Seys, 44.
Shaw, Sir John, 57.
Sheep, 14, 22; prices of, 13, 15, 23; part rent, 22; duty on, 89, 120; taxes on, 95.
Shepherds, 14.
Shepherdland, 20.
Sheriffs, duties belonging to, 84, 86, 93, 152.
Shipping dues, 121, 136; plunder of, 124, 126, 132, 145; protection of, 135; privileges, 132, 142, 145; owned by the towns, 148, 149; tonnage, 148, 149.
Ships, building of, 121, 145; price of, in 1250, 122.
Shirts, of cloth of gold, 32; of silk, 32; bordered, 32.
Silk, regulations concerning, 51; establishment of trade, 52; exemptions, 52; goods, duty on, 99.
Simon of St Andrews, 112.
Sinderit, 39.
Silver maill, 22, 25.
Skene, Mr., 7, 81.
Skins, factory of rabbit and hare, 66; revenue from, 88; sheep skins, ex-

INDEX.

port of, 88, 89, 135, 149 ; revenue from, 89 ; regulation concerning, 117 ; article of trade, 126.
Sluaged, 8, 9, 81, 82.
Soap, 59 ; part rent, 9 ; import of, 60, 136 ; price of, 60 ; patents granted, 60, 61 ; custom on, 60 ; works, 60, 61.
Sorren, 174, 175, 177, 180.
Sorren-more, 174.
Sorren land. See *Sorren*.
Sorryn, 9.
Southesk, Earl of, 145.
Sowing, 4 ; times of, 14.
Spalding Club, 25.
Spark, John, 19.
Spears, import of, 135.
Speir, 45.
Spendings, common, 176.
Spenser, Edmund, 176.
Spey, 69.
Spyner, 40.
Stair, Master of, 50.
St. Andrews, 56, 145.
S. Columba, 4, 7.
S. Columb Cillé, 32.
S. Kentigern, 5.
S. Ninian, 4.
St. Pol and Blois, Earl of, 121.
S. P. 1535, II., 179.
S. P. O. 1550, 177, 178.
S. P. O. 1587 ; *Desmond's Rents and Ware*, 174, 179, 180.
S. P. O. 1589, Sir W. St. Leger, 175, 179.
S. P. O. II., 174, 176.
Stallage, 76.
Stansfield, Colonel, 44, 45.
Staple, 129, 130, 133, 137, 138, 141, 142.
Statuta Gilde, 113 *et seq.*
Staves, barrel, 148.
Steelbow, 6.
Stemmingis, 37.
Stented, 139.
Stewart, Alan, 16.
Stewart, Walter, 16.
Stirling, 54, 56 ; revenue on salmon export, 70; kept standard measures, 157 ; pints, 162.
Stirling, Margate, 28.
Stirling, Viscount, 75.
Strangers, 6, 70, 117.
Strathearn, Earl of, 75.
Strathgrif, 8.
Streets, cleansing of, 117.
Stockings, children taught to knit, 46, 49 ; silk, duty on, 100.

Strowan, 177.
Stuht, 6.
Sugar, works, 63 ; tax on, 63 ; immunities of, 63, import of, 150.
Sunday work, 55.
Supply, 99.
Sutherland, Earl of, 86.
Swine, 14 ; price of, 15 ; part rent, 9, 22, 85 ; paid duty, 120.
Syner, 40.
Syoks, 19.
Tacksmen, 26.
Táin Bo Chuailgne, 31.
Tallow, export of, 135 ; weighing of, 160.
Tanist, The, 7.
Taoiseach, 173.
Tar, 150.
Taverns, 119.
Taxes (see also *Customs, Revenue, Cain, Conveth*, and *Cuddicke*), for teaching weaving, 44, exemptions from, 41, 44, 52, 63, 92 ; on ribbons and thread, 46 ; on glass, 58 ; on sugar, 63 ; on fish, 70, 71 ; Celtic, 79 ; how paid, 80 ; receivers of, 84 ; growing increase of, 88 ; on silver, 91 ; first, 92 ; for national aid, 92, 93, 94 ; on land, 93 ; new, 95 ; general, 96 *et seq.* ; on ships, 106, 107, 121 ; on cattle, horses, and swine, 120.
Tenure of land, 6 ; of tribe-land, 8, 9 ; of cottars, 10, 12, 17; of husbandi, 11, 12 ; by lease, 16-21 ; of crofters, 22 ; feudal, 82, 86.
Terra dominica. See *Demesne*.
Thanages, 81, 84, 85, 86.
Thread, impost on, 46 ; linen, 120.
Thomas, Captain, 169.
Thore, Adam, 91.
Thurlow, Secretary, 98, 101.
Tigherumas, Mac Ollaig, 31.
Timber, import of, 38, 120, 148, 149, 150.
Tobacco, excise rates on, 99.
Toisech, The, 7. See also *Taoisech*.
Tolbooth, 159.
Tome ton, 121.
Torfœus, 108.
Touk of drume, 45.
Town, 10.
Trade, 104 ; monopolies in, 109 ; regulations of Statuta Gilde regarding, 117 ; international methods of, 129 ; with Greenland, 61 ; general foreign, 105, 108, 121 ; 129, 135, 136, 149, 150 ; with

England, 106, 107, 109, 110, 111, 112, 113, 124, 127, 134, 149; with the Netherlands, 107, 108, 111, 127, 129, 130, 132, 135, 137, 140, 141, 148, 149; with Norway, 108, 111, 113, 125, 128, 148, 149, 150; with Ireland, 110, 113, 122, 127, 128; with France, 111, 112, 113, 137, 138, 139, 140, 148; with Wales, 124; with Denmark, 138, 141; with India, 146; with Africa, 146; with West Indies, 149, 150.
Tribes, tenure of land in, 6, 8, 9; headman of, 6; office-bearers of, 7; home-steads, 7; rights of headship, 8; rents in, 8, 9; industries of, 31.
Tron, 152.
Trout. See *Fisheries*.
Tuath, 6, 7.
Tucker, Mr., 56, 100, 101, 146, 148.
Tunic, 32.
Tullibardine, Earl of, 145.
Turnberry, 54.
Turner, James, 58, 66.
Tyrone, Earl of, 173, 178.
Uddart, Nathaniel, 60.
Uddert, Nicholas, 141.
Udny, Laird of, 145.
Ulster Journal of Archæology, 173, 177.
Union, Act of, 57.
Vagabonds, 49; vagrants and, 98.
Valuation Roll, 92, 93.
Vanhort, Abigail, 40.
Vauday, Monks of, 111.
Vduart, Nicolas, 36.
Vegetables, 120.
Wageouris, 80.
Wages, of fishermen, 73; for military service, 95; fixing of, 132.
Waggons, 13.
Waitings, 81.
Walkers, 35, 36.
Warren, 19.
War of Independence, 93.
Wax, 120; stone weight of, 159.
Waytinga. See *Conveth*.
W. Con., 181.
Wealth, of different classes, 94, 95, 96; of Scotland, 105, 106, 107, 108, 110, 121, 126, 127.
Weavers, 35; Incorporation of, in Glasgow, 46.

Wedale, 14.
Weights, 151; reformation of, 152; regulations concerning, 153, 154; unit of, 159; standard, 160, 161.
— Stone, 153, 154, 156; of Lanark, 159, 160; tron stone, 160.
— Pound, 154, 159, 160, 161.
— Tron, 156, 160.
— Troy, 156.
— Ounce, 159, 160.
— Waw, 159.
— Drop, 160.
— Grain, 160.
— Mark, 160.
— Serplath, 160.
— Ton, light, 160.
Weights and Measures, 28.
Weights and Measures of Scotland, Treatise on, 169.
Wemyss, glass work at, 57, 58.
Wergild, 86.
Wheat, 13, 19, 21, 85; prices of, 12, 15; taxes on, 95, 130, 165; import of, 136; as a symbol, 177.
Whiting, 120.
Whittinghame, Laird of, 139.
Wigton, 154, 155.
Wilkin, Archibald, 37.
William de Bowden, 112.
William the Lion, 12, 30, 34, 54, 67, 83, 93, 108, 109, 124.
William III., 99.
William de Marisco, 113.
Wine, excise rates on, 99; trade in, 111, 112, 121, 135, 136, 148, 150.
Websters, 35, 36; Flemish, 36, 37, 39; Dutch, 40, 42.
Wolves, 20.
Women, flyting, 28; married, 118.
Woods, 18.
Wool, prices of, 23; export of, 36, 37, 38, 41, 88; import of, 43; spinning and fining of, 46, 49; revenue from, 90; trade in, 111, 112, 117, 135; duty on, 136; stone weight of, 159, 160.
Woolfells. See *Sheepskins*.
Wrights, Incorporation of, 58.
Wrotham, W. de, 109.
Wylie, James, 28.
Xifiline, 3.
York, Duke of, 46.
Ythan, 69.

www.ingramcontent.com/pod-product-compliance
Lightning Source LLC
Chambersburg PA
CBHW020903230426
43666CB00008B/1297